T0157682

Nu

Nu

A real-life account of two teachers, one Vietnamese and one American, in a small town in the Central Highlands of Vietnam from 1967 to 1969.

James J. Flannery

iUniverse, Inc.

New York   Bloomington

Nu

A real-life account of two teachers, one Vietnamese
and one American, in a small town in the Central
Highlands of Vietnam from 1967 to 1969.

Copyright © 2009 by James J. Flannery

*All rights reserved. No part of this book may be used or reproduced by
any means, graphic, electronic, or mechanical, including photocopying,
recording, taping or by any information storage retrieval system
without the written permission of the publisher except in the case
of brief quotations embodied in critical articles and reviews.*

iUniverse books may be ordered through booksellers or by contacting:

iUniverse
1663 Liberty Drive
Bloomington, IN 47403
www.iuniverse.com
1-800-Authors (1-800-288-4677)

*Because of the dynamic nature of the Internet, any Web addresses or links
contained in this book may have changed since publication and may no longer be
valid. The views expressed in this work are solely those of the author and do not
necessarily reflect the views of the publisher, and the publisher hereby disclaims
any responsibility for them.*

ISBN: 978-1-4401-3193-6 (pbk)
ISBN: 978-1-4401-3194-3 (ebk)

Printed in the United States of America

iUniverse rev. date: 3/25/2009

Foreword

There are many misconceptions about Vietnam. Very few soldiers actually got to know the Vietnamese people. Hollywood painted pictures with a broad brush, attempting to sell films.

This book describes a much different Vietnam, from the perspective of two young schoolteachers, one Vietnamese and one American. They lived in the town of An Tuc, high in the Central Highlands of Vietnam.

This book describes what they did, and what happened to them, for two years, from 1967 to 1969. The people in this book are *real people*, though some names have been changed to protect people who are still there.

Nu

The young school teacher hurried toward the open air market place. Her face showed the strain of worry about her tiny sister, sick with malaria. Perhaps some lime in her sister's tea would help break the fever and give Tuc some relief. On her way to a stand that had limes, she picked up some basil and ginger root from another vendor. "This may help her appetite, and settle her stomach." She picked up two limes, and prepared to cross the paved highway.

"Nu! Lai, xin!"

Nu turned and headed towards a group of students, to answer their question. It took just moments, and she headed across the road with the handful of groceries. It was only a four minute walk from the market to the home she shared with her sister and the elderly couple that hosted them in An Tuc.

"Tuc is smiling," said Aunt, as she fanned Tuc with a wicker hand-held fan. Uncle was washing Tuc's naked body with a wet cloth. Nu smiled, relieved, and handed the produce to Aunt, as she took over the duties of fanning Tuc.

Nu

"The lime may help bring her fever down. Put some in her tea, and we can give her thin slices with her pho. There is plenty for all of us."

Aunt turned and dropped some noodles in the broth that was already simmering. It would just take a couple of minutes for the noodles to cook. She then sliced the ginger root and dropped about twenty thin slices into the broth to flavor the noodles. She spread several bowls on the bed, with the basil, some mung sprouts, chilies, cilantro and julienne vegetables. By the time those were spread out, the noodles were cooked. Aunt passed a bowl of pho and chopsticks to Nu, Tuc and Uncle. She would fan them while they ate, then she would eat her pho.

As Nu ate, she watched Tuc carefully, and conversed with Aunt and Uncle. Tuc was hungry, and looking much better than she had for the past week. The fever had done its work, killing a generation of the adult malaria parasite. Tuc would be all right until another generation of the parasite grew in her liver and attacked her bloodstream. They would all be able to sleep well tonight.

"Drink more cha. Drink as much as you can, and put lime in it for your fever." Tuc drank two cups, but then quickly moved toward the door. She had to urinate. Nu saw that she was still very unsure on her feet, so she rushed over to help Tuc across the flats to an area used for that purpose. Tuc squatted, but was glad to have Nu's knees to hold on to. Nu also squatted, then pulled her black silk pants back up and put Tuc on her hip to carry back down to the house. For the last week, Tuc hadn't been able to go to the flats, and had to urinate in the night chamber pot under the bed.

By the time they got back, Aunt had already eaten, and was finishing the cleanup. Lunch was simple, and easy to both cook and clean up.

Nu turned to Uncle. "Get some sleep. I will fan Tuc for a while, then take my nap." Siesta was a part of life in rural Vietnam, because the sun was brutal in the afternoon.

Flight to Saigon

Jim looked at the Thai stewardess, and answered, "Anything that is very cold, please. With extra ice." The stewardess gave him a choice of several beverages, and he chose Coke. He was still very sweaty from spending three hours at the open-air terminal in Manilla while the plane was fueled and restocked with supplies. It had been the middle of the night, but Manilla was like a steam bath. Jim needed a shower very badly.

"Heading to Saigon?" Jim looked at the man next to him, who had been reading "QST", a magazine for Ham Radio Operators. "Initially, yes, but I'm not sure where to head after that. I'm hoping to find some nice town somewhere and get a job, teaching school."

"You're the adventurous type then. I figured you must be. Name's Dave. Dave Guthrie. I just spent two years installing telephone equipment for the Army in An Khe. That's about 400 clicks north of Saigon."

Jim shook Dave's hand. "Jim Flannery. I just graduated from Penn State. I had to work my way through, so I didn't graduate until August. That was too late to land a position for this year, so I figured I might as well get some practical experience. I noticed you were reading "QST", so I figured you were another Ham." They exchanged call signs, and the stewardess returned with their breakfast.

"This Thai airline sure feeds you well!"

"You'll find that all over Asia. Quality food, quality service. Not like the U.S. airlines. Vietnamese food is hard to beat. Thai food is even better, if you don't mind real hot chili peppers! Vietnamese is much milder than Thai. Hey, what kind of town are you looking for in Vietnam?"

"Hopefully some place that's cooler than Manilla!"

"Manilla is as bad as it gets. You might like where I was. It is high in the mountains. It gets real hot in the day, but the nights are comfy, and it is very very dry."

"That sure sounds good to me. Can you draw me a map of how to get there?"

As Dave drew the map, he asked, "Any idea where you'll stay in Saigon tonight?"

"I'll probably find a hotel somewhere. Any suggestions?"

"Yes. The U.S. Army has a lot of hotels in Saigon. I stay at the Metropol, where a lot of the reporters stay. Right across the street is the Rex B.O.Q. That is for officers. There's an open mess on the roof where you can get free meals and free drinks and enjoy the view."

"Free sounds just fine with me!"

Nu

"It is on Tu-Do Street, the main drag. The central market is just a few blocks south, and the palace is a few blocks past that. It is kind of like Pennsylvania Ave. in D. C. Be very careful of your wallet down there. You'll be okay in the countryside, but Saigon is full of thieves. I'll take you to the Metropol."

Saigon

Dave gestured out the window. "Take the window seat, Jim." They exchanged seats, and Jim watched the coastline come into view. The South China Sea was very shallow, and Jim could see fishing boats working nets below. Farther ahead, islands came into view, and the sandy coastline. The Thai airliner was gradually losing altitude to come in for a landing at Tan Son Nhut Airport, which was both the civilian airport and an American Air Force Base. It took longer to reach than Jim anticipated. They flew over many towns, with palm trees and people going about their daily activities. It looked very peaceful. There was no sign of war.

Jim stuck close to Dave going through the terminal and Customs. Customs simply stamped their passports with no questions asked. They quickly picked their way through the crowd outside, and past a guarded gate, onto the outside street. Dave flagged down a gray U. S. Navy station wagon, and said, "Metropol." When the station wagon was full, it headed quickly into traffic. "Just like a cab, Jim." "Pretty neat!"

The road was filled with mostly bicycles, motor scooters, and electric Bendix bikes. There seemed to be no traffic control at all on the city streets. Most of the scooters were very smoky. Many of the people on the streets were just cruising, for fun. Jim laughed when he saw a scooter with two girls, and the girl on back was holding an umbrella over both people. It didn't take long to see another, and yet another. This was quite common. Dave saw Jim marveling at this sight, and explained, "Very light skin is important, especially for girls. They try to keep the sun off themselves."

"Our stop!" Dave and Jim hopped out by a sidewalk bunker, guarding the entrance to the Hotel Metropol. There were two Vietnamese soldiers in the bunker, which was constructed of several layers of sand bags, with a large umbrella over top. They quickly went inside, and to the registration desk. An American soldier checked them in, and handed each a key, a towel and a bar of soap. "It is almost dinnertime. Meet me in the lobby in a half hour and we'll go to the Rex."

"Make it 45 minutes, Dave. I need a shower badly."

"45 it is."

The room was quite spacious, with two large ceiling fans. There seemed to be air conditioning of sorts, but it was still quite warm. Jim opened his suitcase and backpack, and took out fresh clothes. He had packed lightly, with two spare shirts and two spare pair of shorts and underwear. Shedding his travel clothes, he headed toward the bathroom. He was in desperate need of the toilet. "Uh oh. What the hell is this?" Instead of a toilet, there was a ceramic square on the floor, whose purpose was obvious, but how to use it was not immediately apparent. The square was less than a metre square, with two raised ceramic footprints, and a plain pipe located between the heels of the footprints. There was nothing to hold on to, no toilet paper, and no flush handle. Next to the square, was a large can, filled with water. After studying the device, Jim placed his feet on the footprints, and lowered himself to a squatting position over the pipe. The procedure worked well. "This is just what dogs do. Oh well!"

Stepping into the shower, Jim noted that there was only one water temperature. Only one faucet: cold. "Oh well!" He would have this thought often. The shower felt good after all the sweating he had done, and he felt refreshed when he was done. He stepped to the sink to brush his teeth, and saw instructions in both Vietnamese and French. He quickly determined that the instructions were to advise him that the water was not potable. "I wonder if it is okay to brush my teeth with it." Not seeing any other source of water, he brushed his teeth.

Dave was already waiting in the lobby when Jim got off the elevator. "What did you think, Jim?"

"I've never seen a toilet like that before, Dave. I figured you put your feet on the footprints and squat?"

"Yes. The can of water next to it is how you flush. When you get out in the countryside, you'll just find yourself a comfy spot of ground and do the same thing. One thing to note, is the lower you squat, the better it works. You don't even need toilet paper if you squat low enough."

"The sign on the sink says not to drink the water?"

"Yes. There are no water treatment plants here. The Navy has a desalination plant, and delivers water in tankers. It should be good, but they pump it to a tank on the roof, and you can't be sure what else goes into the tank."

They got off the elevator one floor below the roof of the Rex B.O.Q. Grabbing trays, they worked their way through the line, picking out their dinner from a limited selection. It wasn't great cuisine, but it wasn't bad looking. "We can bring this up to the roof and enjoy the scenery while we eat." Taking the stairs, Jim noticed that there was a television in another room, and the programming was in Vietnamese. It appeared to be an operatic play.

On the roof, they found perhaps a hundred tables. Most were occupied, and Jim noticed that most of the people appeared to be American civilians. "Are these people reporters?"

"Yes, most are. If you get questioned while traveling, just act like you are a reporter, and you can go most anywhere you like. They go to the daily briefing at five o'clock at MACV headquarters, come back here, add a little moxie to it, and send it back to their bosses in the States. For that, they get paid really well, and live here for free. Even the booze is free."

"MACV?"

"Military Assistance Command, Vietnam. Army headquarters. Supposedly this is Vietnam's war, and we are just here to help."

Dave and Jim conversed most of the evening, watching the sun set, and picking up bits of conversations from nearby tables. After sunset, they could see flares in the distance, dropped from helicopters or airplanes. No shooting, just flares to light up certain areas.

"I have a couple of busy days tying up loose ends and lots of paperwork before heading off for Nigeria."

"Nigeria?"

"My work is done here, and I've landed a contract with Nigerian Telecom to install some modern telephone switchers in Lagos and Port Harcourt. I'll see more war there than here in Vietnam."

"Why do you do this?"

"The money is very very good, Jim."

They got up, and made their way down to the street. "There's a curfew in the entire country at sundown. We can walk across to the hotel, but we can't go anywhere else." Jim nodded understanding, but was tired, and didn't say anything. When they got to the elevator, they bid each other goodnight, and went to their rooms.

A Full Day In Saigon

Jim slept under the ceiling fan, but awakened perspiring, so he hit the shower before heading out. Stopping at the hotel desk, he said he would be staying at least until tomorrow. He needed coffee, so he headed straight across to the Rex. The sun was too strong on the roof, so he stayed in the mess hall and drank three cups of coffee.

On the street, Jim decided to see Saigon and get a feel for the country. Heading down Tu-Do street, Jim noted that the street signs were either in French or a combination of French and Vietnamese. "Rue Tu-Do" assured him that he was on the right street. The sidewalks were wide, with tables for people to enjoy their breakfast and read their morning newspapers. Between the sidewalk cafés, people had set up wares to sell right on the sidewalk. Some of the things were new, but many were used, and probably stolen. Vendors tried to get Jim's attention, offering everything from watches to whores.

After several blocks, Jim passed the Central Market, a huge building filled with individual stalls selling produce, meat, fish, live chickens, eels, snakes, radios, clothing, and most anything you might want. The market smelled strongly of fish, and was very noisy. After a brief look,

Jim continued down the street. There were signs and billboards everywhere, with writing in Vietnamese, French, Chinese and English.

Crossing a street, Jim stopped abruptly, looking into a Volkswagen showroom. The centerpiece was a Volkswagen camper. It looked so very out of place in the middle of Saigon. Jim's mind raced with the possibilities that the camper would give him. It could be a place for him to live, as well as being transportation. It had a folding bed, a sink, a stove and a real toilet. He would have to think about this.

A couple of more blocks, and he passed the Presidential Palace. It was heavily guarded, but didn't seem too secure in case of an attack.

Continuing his walk down Tu-Do Street, Jim saw the signs change. Now they were mostly in Chinese. He was in the city of Cholon, an ethnic Chinese city in the heart of Saigon. Who were these Chinese, and why were they in Vietnam?

Turning around, Jim tried to absorb everything he saw. There were only a few cars. Bicycles, motorcycles, scooters, Lambros, and Bendix bikes were everywhere. If he got the Volkswagen camper, would he find a dealership to keep it running? He decided it would be too impractical. A small motorcycle would do very nicely.

Back in downtown Saigon, Jim found a sidewalk café with an awning for protection from the sun. He had to wait for a table to clear, so he observed the patrons.

Nu

They were mostly European or American civilians. None seemed rushed or concerned. They slowly savored their lunches. Every European language was spoken, as far as he could tell. He was glad to get a small table near a group of French and a group of Germans. He listened, and picked up pieces of the conversations. This would be a safe place to eat, judging by the large number of Europeans eating here. Jim watched trays of food being brought out, and picked out a plate that smelled wonderful as it went by.

A waiter came to take his order, and Jim pointed to the plate he had picked out. "I'll have what he is having, and coffee, please."

"Certainly." The waiter spoke English. That was reassuring.

The coffee was brought immediately, and was a surprise. It was delivered with a small tin drip pot sitting on top of a glass with sweetened condensed milk in the bottom. The coffee slowly dripped into the condensed milk. There was a small teapot as well, that held hot water. When the drip pot was empty, you could add more hot water to make more coffee. There was another glass, with ice cubes. You could have your coffee hot or iced. Jim added water, and watched as it dripped into the condensed milk. No wonder people don't seem to be in a hurry here. It takes so long to brew a cup of coffee.

Taking the tin drip device off the glass, Jim stirred the coffee with the condensed milk. It took a while. The milk was very thick. Jim was about to pour the coffee into the glass of ice cubes when a German at the next table stopped him. "Nein! Vorsicht! Es ist nicht potable."

"Danke!"

"Are you American?"

"Yes. I just got here, and am learning the ropes."

"Well, never trust ice or water. You don't know where it came from. Drink tea, coffee or beer, or anything that is boiled or comes in a bottle that hasn't been opened."

Setting the spoon aside, Jim took a sip of the coffee. "Wow! This coffee is great!" He turned to his German neighbor, who smiled.

"Yes. I am in the coffee business. I buy coffee here and ship it to Europe. This coffee is made from the Robusta cherry, not the Arabica."

"Well, I've never tasted anything like it. I've never imagined that coffee could be this good. Did you say cherry?"

"Yes, it is grown around the city of Dalat, about 200 kilometres north of here, then roasted at Buon Me Thuot, and we ship it from Saigon by plane and boat to Europe. Coffee beans are the pit of a tropical cherry tree."

The waiter brought lunch, and Jim ordered another coffee. Lunch was exceptionally good, but the coffee made anything worthwhile. He was going to enjoy this.

Sin City

After lunch, Jim decided to take a nap and spend the evening on the rooftop bar at the Rex, to learn as much as he could. Walking on the sidewalk, a scooter passed very close, and Jim felt his watch slide off his wrist, onto the finger of the passenger on the scooter. The passenger looked back at Jim, laughing. He was very good at his trade. He was a thief.

"You had an expansion band on that watch. Very easy to slip off." It was an American soldier that had been walking behind Jim. "Saigon is Sin City. Everybody has something going, Sir. Guard everything you have, and be alert at all times."

"Thank you."

Jim entered the Metropol, and went up to his room. He brushed his teeth and took a shower, then laid under the fan to take a nap.

Later that evening, he went to the rooftop at the Rex, and struck up conversations with several of the civilians there. Most were reporters, some were contractors to the Army. He learned as much as he could from all the people he met. He would have to adapt to this place in order to survive. He learned that he could get anything he wanted just by telling a street vendor what he needed. He decided to try to get a motorcycle the next day.

In the morning, Jim packed up his backpack and discarded the suitcase. He would travel even lighter than when he flew here. There were a few items he knew he wouldn't need now that he had seen Saigon.

Down on the street, vendors tried to sell him watches, radios, and souvenirs. "You want my sister?"

"I want a motorcycle."

"How big?"

"150 CC or more."

"You wait here."

"I'll wait at this café and have some coffee."

"Good, Sir! Enjoy your coffee. I come back soon."

It was worth a shot. The man seemed confident that he could produce a motorcycle. Jim was on his second cup of roasted heaven when the man reappeared, riding a Honda 175 CC motorcycle that looked fairly new. He revved the bike, and it sounded good. "You like this one? It is almost new."

"How much?"

"Four hundred dollars MPC or forty thousand Piasters."

MPC were "Military Payment Certificates", which represented dollars, but their design would change periodically to thwart the black market. Jim saw his opportunity.

"I can give you real American dollars instead of MPC, but only three hundred." Real dollars were in great demand, so Jim had the man where he wanted him. Also, the man was sweating. He didn't want to stand around with a hot bike, arguing. He wanted the money and he wanted to get out of the area quickly.

"Yes. Good."

Jim handed him the money, and the man melted into the crowd. Jim threw on his backpack, and quickly drove the motorcycle three blocks off Tu-Do Street. He turned north, and paralleled Tu-Do out of Saigon. He didn't stop until he had passed several small towns, and found a sparsely inhabited area near a beach, with lots of foliage to hide the bike and examine it. His conscience gnawed at him, but he was just following the local lifestyle.

After relieving himself in the bushes, Jim examined the bike. It was probably less than six months old, and in very good condition. There was no license plate. He tried to remember whether other motorcycles had plates, but he could visualize them both with and without plates. He would have to pay attention as he went up the road. He checked the gas tank and oil. The oil was full and clean. The gas tank was half full. He couldn't remember seeing a gas station anywhere in Saigon or along Highway 1.

A brief swim in the South China Sea was refreshing.

The water was very warm. Almost bath warm. Jim felt clean. He pushed the bike out of the shrubbery, and continued northward. At times, the road was near the beach, with fishing villages, and at other times it was more inland. There were many bridges over streams. At each bridge, Jim saw a bunker guarded by Vietnamese soldiers. They were guarding the bridges to keep this most important of roads open. It was a good road, recently paved.

Entering a medium sized town, Jim saw a couple of Lambros carrying passengers. Jim knew they had to get gas from somewhere, so he pulled up beside a parked Lambro, pointed to his gas tank, and said, "Gas? Petrol?" The young man nodded a yes, and went inside a building to get a gas can. It took a little more than a gallon to fill the tank, and Jim gave the man fifty Piasters. That was good.

Jim saw a café ahead, and stopped for lunch. The selection here was limited to noodle soup with greens and veggies, but no meat. At least they had the heavenly roast that Jim had come to love in Saigon.

Heading up the coast, Jim noticed schoolgirls wearing the traditional formal dress that he would learn was called Ao Dai. It consisted of a tunic top with an ankle length front and back panel, split at the waist. On the bottom, they wore either white or black silk pants. The front and back panels flowed as the girls walked, and made them look like graceful angels. It was hard to take his eyes off them. Their hair was striking as well. It was jet black, shiny, and very straight. It almost always extended beyond their bums as if it was trying to grow clear to the ground. It was a coarse hair that would not easily curl.

Jim also noticed a change in demographics as he left Saigon. There were lots of men in Saigon, but north of the city it was hard to find young men. There were elderly men in the fields, and little boys in town, but very few young men.

Night On The Beach

Riding north along Highway 1, Jim again bought gas as he went through a medium sized town. He hadn't seen a hotel in any of the towns that he passed through. Where would he stay? He only had a couple of hours till sundown, and he would be stopped by the curfew. He needed to find a place to stay for the night. He had no idea how far Qui Nhon was, where he would turn to go to An Khe. He decided that he would look for an area near the beach with foliage to hide in and to conceal the bike. A sudden worry crossed his mind, that the Viet Cong might also look for such a place. He certainly didn't want to just drive into an enemy camp! Weighing his choices, he didn't see any alternative. It would be the beach.

From the top of a hill, he could see that the road went along the beach ahead, and there was lots of foliage. He didn't see any towns in that stretch. He would turn off the engine and quietly coast to a likely spot, then remain in cover till it was completely dark. Jim put the bike in neutral, and killed the engine. Coasting, he went slower and slower as he reached the flats. There! Just ahead, he saw a grove of coconut palms with ground cover, near the water's edge. Perfect! He had run out of momentum, and had to dismount and push the bike a short distance to reach the grove. There was nobody around. Good.

The sand felt good, and Jim laid in it, using his backpack as a pillow. He napped until the sun was completely down. When he couldn't see his hand in front of him any more, he shed his clothes, walked into the water, and relieved himself. Walking farther into the water, he bathed as best he could. The water felt warm and good. Back on the beach, he had trouble finding the bike and backpack, but eventually stubbed his toe on the backpack. He laid down, and listened very carefully for any sound that might be Viet Cong. He heard nothing, and eventually fell asleep. The sand was soft, the breeze gentle, and he slept well.

Nora Hadley

In the morning, Jim took another relief break and bath in the South China Sea, and headed north again. The countryside grew more rugged, but Highway 1 was still an excellent road. A couple of U. S. Army convoys passed in the other direction, and Jim eventually overtook one heading north. When they stopped, he pulled up to a truck, and asked how far it was to Qui Nhon. The soldier said about an hour or two. Jim got some gas from them and continued on his way. The road hugged the beach on the right, and on the left side, there was a steep cliff. The rocks were totally covered in foliage, and looked very pretty. This was a beautiful country.

At about noon, the cliff retreated back from the road, and a broad valley opened up ahead. A road sign confirmed that this was Qui Nhon. It was a large port city. Entering Qui Nhon, Jim saw an American Army base, and stopped near the entrance, wondering if he should go in and grab some lunch.

"Lost?"

Jim turned to see an American woman driving an

Army jeep. She wore a blue dress, very short, with a Red Cross patch on the sleeve.

"Not lost, really. Just wondering if I'd be welcome here to grab some lunch before heading to An Khe."

"Well, follow me to the mess hall, and you're my guest."

She went through the gate, and Jim followed her to the mess hall. It was air conditioned, and felt really good. Before going in, they made cursory introductions. They'd get better acquainted over lunch.

"Nora Hadley. I'm the Red Cross Hospital Field Director here."

"Jim Flannery. I'm heading up to An Khe to see about working as a school teacher there."

They got trays of food, and Jim drank several iced teas to wash the road dust out of his system. Before they realized, it was late afternoon, and people were coming in the mess hall for dinner.

"It takes three hours to get to An Khe. You won't make it before sundown. I can get you a B.O.Q. for the night here, and you can head out in the morning."

"Sounds good."

Jim followed Nora's jeep towards the beach. They turned into a complex of lovely stucco beach houses directly across from the beach. There was no sign of bunkers or other security anywhere in sight. Jim followed

Nora into an office, and they gave Jim a key without question.

"These villas were a French resort. Vietnam hasn't closed to tourists, and there are many lovely areas where Europeans still come to vacation. The Army took these over as housing. You won't need to do any laundry or make your bed in the morning. We have real maid service here."

They said good-night, and Jim went into his villa. It was gorgeous! Just like a resort anywhere in the world. The hot water faucet gave hot water, and there was a real toilet!

Road To An Tuc

"Rise and shine, Jim! We can have breakfast before you head out."

"I'm already up and packed, Nora. Thanks for yesterday! Breakfast sounds good, and I need to find some gas to get up to An Khe."

"I've got gas in the can on my jeep. I also made a list of some people for you to look up in An Khe. They can probably help you get things you need."

"Hey thanks!"

At breakfast, Nora gave Jim the list of people, and also a map to An Khe. She explained that the real town was An Tuc, and that the soldiers weren't allowed to go to An Tuc, to keep it from being corrupted. "After you cross the bridge, you'll be in An Khe. It is mostly trinket dealers, steam baths, massages, and whore houses. That is why the soldiers aren't supposed to go into An Tuc." She went on to say that there was a Catholic church and school in An Khe, and an independent schoolteacher in An Tuc. "When you get to the center of Qui Nhon, you'll see a sign for Route 19 to Pleiku. An Khe is half way to Pleiku. It is about three hours."

Finishing breakfast, Jim said, "I really want to thank you for all your hospitality, Nora. I'll be sure to look you up when I pass through Qui Nhon."

"Just be sure to let me know how things worked out for you!"

Jim drove into Qui Nhon, easily found the sign to Pleiku, and turned west, towards the mountains. The broad valley gradually narrowed, as the road climbed a gentle slope. There were a few small towns along the way, and lots of terraced farm land where rice was grown. It was a pastoral scene. On the north side of the road, there was a large stone temple. "Probably Buddhist," Jim thought. As he approached the end of the valley, he could see several tents, several hundred metres to the north of the road, with the Red Cross symbol on the tent roofs. There was no military to be seen in the area.

The road was very good, with fairly new asphalt, but it was getting steep. Jim approached a sign in French, that said, "Vitesse, lacettes 15 kMh". He almost ran off the road while trying to translate the sign. He knew that vitesse meant "slow". Now he knew that lacettes were switchbacks. Even 15 kMh was fast on these switchbacks. This road would be dangerous!

The road climbed through switchbacks for almost a half hour. At times, he would look back down, and realize that one false move would hurtle him through the sky to a certain death far below. The foliage thinned as he approached the top, and he noted that the foliage was mostly scrub and cactus now.

At the top, there was a white tent with two large silk flies for shade. Two Vietnamese girls sat in the tent, and had first aid equipment and water. He stopped.

"Hello, do you speak English?"

"Yes, a little English." They offered him water, saying that it was boiled water, and safe to drink. He accepted. "We are here in case of crash. We help." Jim thanked them, and asked how far it was to An Khe. "Thirty minutes, I think."

Continuing, Jim noticed that the land was semi-arid. Not much grew at all. To the north and to the south were mountains with trees on the upper slopes. The road was level and straight now, climbing gently. After a while, he saw trees in the distance, and terraced farmland. This would be An Tuc. He slowed, carefully surveying the area. It looked like a good sized town, with lots of rice paddies, trees, and a very large open-air market. He eased the bike toward the market, and killed the engine.

"Are you American?"

"Yes. My name is Jim. I am a school teacher."

The girl's face brightened. "Hello Sim!" She didn't get the pronunciation right, but Jim didn't correct her. Turning, she said something to the other children, and several went running off, to get someone. Jim would wait to see what might happen.

Greeting

Several children were coming back now. In front, was a wisp of a girl, who looked to be about nine or ten years old. She was emaciated. Jim could see the outline of her rib bones through her white shirt. She was also half bald. Like other girls, she had very long black hair, but there wasn't much of it. The sun glistened off her unprotected scalp. She needed a hat, but wasn't wearing one.

Something about the way she walked towards Jim caught his attention. She walked directly towards him, confidently. Her gait had obvious purpose.

As she walked toward Jim, Nu was sizing him up. He was about average size for an American. His closely cropped beard told her that he wasn't a soldier. What would bring him to An Tuc?

She walked directly up to Jim, extended her hand, and said, "Hello, you are an American school teacher?"

Still thinking that this girl was only nine or ten years old, Jim said, "Yes. My name is Jim. I am hoping to meet your teacher. Your English sounds very good, so you must have a very good teacher."

Nu

Nu laughed, "Thank you! I am the teacher here. My name is Nu. Spelled N U, pronounced Noo." She picked up a stick and drew her name in the dirt of the marketplace.

Jim was shocked, and blurted out, "How old are you?" He regretted the way that sounded, but couldn't take it back.

"I am nineteen years. I have been the teacher here for two years."

Jim didn't know what to say. This was such a surprise, that he stood speechless. He wanted to say something, but nothing came to mind.

"Mister Jim, perhaps you would like to join me for lunch? We can get acquainted."

Thankful that Nu had rescued him from his silence, Jim gratefully accepted. She turned, and Jim followed, pushing the bike. They crossed Highway 19, and turned onto a dirt road that paralleled the river, starting at the bridge. At the third dirt alley to the left, they turned and walked up to a small mud and stick hut. It was just like every other house, about three metres square, with a doorway, but no door. There were no windows. The roof was steep, and was made of very thick straw. Inside, there was only one piece of furniture, which served as bed, table and chair. There was only a narrow strip on two sides to walk around the bed. The floor was dirt, but swept clean. The only decoration was a small, colorful Buddhist altar on the wall.

"Jim, I would like to introduce Uncle and Aunt." Jim held out his hand, and they both shook it. Nu spoke to Aunt in Vietnamese, and Aunt reached under the bed, pulling out a box. She retrieved one bowl, and went outside to the cooking area, adding more water to a pot that was cooking on a charcoal hibachi.

"This is my sister, Tuc. She is five years."

"Hello Tuc."

Tuc smiled, then turned to Nu, and they had a brief conversation. Nu sat on the bed, and motioned that Jim should sit down. Aunt came in, and arranged several bowls on the bed, where everyone could reach. Then she brought more bowls with noodle soup, and a glass filled with chopsticks. There were no spoons. Everyone grabbed a bowl of noodle soup, and began lifting noodles into their mouths with the chopsticks, slurping the broth directly from the bowl. The extra bowls, located between them had various greens and sprouts, to have with the soup. Between bites of noodles, each person would take a sprig of cilantro, or of basil, or some sprouts. Jim put a little of each in his bowl, and tried to stir them into the noodles.

"You don't understand our food, Jim? I will have to show you how to eat. Watch me. If you put the leaves or sprouts in your soup, they will get soft, and won't be good. Eat them separately. To enjoy your pho, every bite should be different, not the same. Here is how to eat with sticks." Nu held the chopsticks, and showed what fingers each stick should rest against. Jim tried it, but it would take some getting used to. Nu pulled a noodle off Jim's beard, and handed him a rag to wipe away the broth.

"I guess this will take a while to develop some skill,"

Jim said, as he wiped his beard. Aunt had removed the empty bowls, and brought tea and sliced fruits in more bowls. "I would like to learn things like how to thank Aunt for lunch."

"Thank you is said, 'Cam ong.'"

Jim turned to Aunt, and smiled. "Cam ong."

Aunt responded, "Khong ca chi."

Nu looked at Jim, and explained, "Khong ca chi is precisely like saying 'Don't mention it' in English. The Chinese would say, 'Bu ke chi'. You see how similar Chinese is to Vietnam? Many of our words are the same or similar. Vietnam language is more formal than Chinese, though. As I teach you how to speak Vietnam, I will also teach you Chinese."

"Why Chinese?"

"For several reasons. First, it will be easy to explain phrases if I explain them in the context of a family of languages. Also, there are many Chinese in Vietnam. It will be good for you to know how to talk with the Chinese. Also, if the V.C. come, you should find Chinese people. They will help you escape."

"Why will Chinese help me?"

"Because our Chinese people escaped the Communists in China. They hate Communists. They would never cooperate with the V.C. In Saigon, the city of Cholon is Chinese. The V.C. never go there."

Now Jim understood why there was such a large Chinese population. "Are there V.C. here?"

"Perhaps, but we never have trouble here. These people are farmers. They have to work hard to eat. Saigon is far, far away, and governments are not important here."

Nu's comment was very reassuring. She had been very matter-of-fact. Jim was convinced.

"Will you show me your school?"

Nu laughed. "You walked through it in the market. There is no school building. The students work as groups, and learn from people experienced in each discipline. My work is to question and direct and evaluate. My school is very much like we learn at the university." With that, Nu reached under the bed and pulled out a suitcase with a few books and papers. She carefully unwrapped plastic from a large book, and handed Jim a diploma. It was written in Vietnamese and French. Though Jim's French was poor, he was able to see that this was a diploma conferring a doctoral degree in linguistics. It was dated 1965.

"You have a Doctorate in linguistics?"

"Yes."

"And you were just seventeen when you received this?"

"Yes. We don't have as much structure as in Europe. We work towards proficiency. When we achieve proficiency, we move on to attain proficiency in other disciplines. I have never gone to a real school. My teacher was my nanny, in Saigon."

"So you are from Saigon, not An Tuc?"

"Yes. My father is a doctor at the government hospital in Saigon."

"And your mother?"

"She was a doctor there too, but she died when Tuc was born. I was with her when she died. It was horrible. Tuc was coming out backwards," Nu patted her rump, "and my father tried to turn her around in the womb. He couldn't. All at once, all of my mother's blood came out, and she died. My father and I were screaming, but he took a scalpel and delivered Tuc. She was blue. Father and I worked on her until she was able to breathe on her own. Then we cried for a long time." Nu's face was contorted in pain, and tears welled up and rolled down her cheeks, soaking her shirt. Jim cried too. Aunt and Uncle knew what Nu had just told Jim. "Come, we will relieve ourselves and then take siesta." Nu took Jim and Tuc by the hand, and headed out the door and up onto the dry flats.

"This is not Saigon. There are no bathrooms here. There is no privacy. It took me a while to get used to it." Jim nodded, and moved a short distance away from Nu and Tuc to relieve himself.

On the way back to the house, Nu explained that Aunt and Uncle were not related to her. She called them Aunt and Uncle as a form of respect for their hosting her. "Hosting the school teacher brings them great status in town, and the town shares food with us. I get no pay, but I am well fed, and need nothing."

"School is only in the morning. There is no work after lunch, because it is too hot. Everyone takes a nap in the afternoon. Do you call that siesta?"

"Yes. We adopted the Spanish word siesta. We don't take siestas in America, but we know what they are."

Aunt and Uncle were already lying down, resting. The bed was almost as large as the house, so Nu took a position with Aunt and Uncle, and Tuc motioned for Jim to lie next to her.

"Jim, you probably noticed that Tuc talks like a baby. She will always talk like a baby. She was without oxygen for too long, so she will never be smart. We can only work to keep her happy and healthy. She gets very sick from malaria, and some day she will not survive. I have devoted my life to taking care of her. She is the last thing that I have of my mother, and I love her very much."

"I understand." Tuc was smiling at Jim. She seemed like a very happy child, despite retardation.

Tuc patted Jim on the belly, and said, "Mop!"

Nu laughed. "Tuc says you are fat."

Remembering the word for "No", Jim laughed good-naturedly, and said, "Khong mop!" They all giggled.

Siesta

A group of children had followed Nu and Jim from the market, and had been ever-present at the doorway during lunch, and until now. Nu spoke to them, and they vanished.

"Those are some of my students. They are learning English, and have been listening to us talk. I told them that we will rest now. They will follow us around as much as they can."

"I had wondered why we always had an audience."

"Jim, tomorrow I will take you to An Khe. There is another school there. It is a Catholic school with real books and real classrooms. You should choose if you would like to work with me, or with them. They can pay you. I can't."

"It will give me a lot to think about."

They all dozed while the merciless sun beat on the straw roof. It was very quiet, as everyone else was taking siesta too. Jim watched tiny lizards scurrying across the roof and walls. The lizards were very good at catching any insect that came inside. Jim dozed.

Dinner

Jim was awakened abruptly by the sound of a dog fight outside. Several children ran by to break up the fight. The dogs had scuffled over a scrap of food. Once it was settled, they each found a patch of shade, and quieted down. Jim was perspiring, and went up to the flats to relieve himself. There were several other people doing the same. When he returned, Aunt was stirring boiling rice in a cast iron kettle on the hibachi outside. She took the kettle off, and set it aside, covered. It would continue to cook without flame for another half hour. That would give Aunt time to collect some greens and veggies for dinner.

"Nu, you don't eat dog here, do you?"

"Never! I am aware of that rumor, but dogs are pets here, just like in America. We also have armadillos as pets. Actually, we seldom have any meat. Chickens and ducks are too important for eggs. We will have meat at New Years, but not much the rest of the year. New Years is in early February. We call it 'Tet'. We use the western calendar for business, but the moon calendar for celebrations and to figure out planting."

Nu

Aunt was passing out bowls of rice, and had bowls of lettuce and julienne veggies and sauces laid out on the centre of the bed. Nu showed Jim how to wrap veggies in the lettuce, to dip in the sauces. One of the sauces was especially tasty, being both sweet and salty. "This sauce is wonderful. What is it?"

"We call it nuouc mam, or fish water in English. It is actually fish wine, made by fermenting tiny, very strong tasting and salty fish."

"Anchovies?"

"Yes. Anchovies. It is very strong, so we mix boiled water and sugar to make the sauce. For the people who live far from the sea, it is a major source of protein. Other sources of protein are mung sprouts and beans.

"I have to find a place to stay. Is there a hotel in An Tuc or An Khe?"

"I already talked with Aunt and Uncle. They would be honored to have you stay here. It would give them great status in town."

"Your home is too small for all of us."

"No! As you saw at siesta, there is plenty of room on the bed for all of us. I will sleep with Aunt and Uncle, and you sleep by the door with Tuc."

Culture Shock

Shortly before sundown, Aunt and Uncle disappeared for a while. Nu and Tuc talked with Jim, asking many questions about America. Several of Nu's students stood in the doorway, listening, and were invited to join in. When Aunt and Uncle came back, their hair was wet, and it was obvious they had been bathing.

"We had better hurry for our bath before sundown." Nu and Tuc took Jim by the hand and they headed toward the river. About half the town's population was already bathing, and Jim guessed there must be two thousand people in or by the river. Jim noticed that they got in the water with their clothes on, but took each garment off, washed it, and hung it on shrubbery by the river's edge to dry. Then they washed themselves. "There is no privacy, Jim. You will have to get used to it like I did."

"Where can I put my wallet and passport so they'll be safe?"

"I should have told you to leave them at home. This isn't Saigon. They should be safe here in your shoes."

Jim didn't know what to do about bathing with two

thousand other people, so he walked into the river and started washing one garment at a time, like the locals did. He felt very awkward being naked in public. When he walked out to drape his shorts over a bush to dry, a group of girls nearby started laughing. Nu splashed them with water, and chastised them for their giggles.

"They are laughing because you have erection. They make joke wondering who excites you. I told them that you come from the city where people don't bathe together, and are embarrassed."

"Thank you. I tried not to have an erection, but that isn't something that a man can easily control."

"Oh I know, and I think they know too, but they have fun with you. They don't mean anything bad."

After bathing, Jim quickly threw his clothes on. Nu and Tuc just walked out of the water and put theirs on. Jim noticed that Nu did have breasts, but they were very small. She only had a few pubic hairs, so the malaria that left her almost bald also limited all her hair. She wasn't concerned about being seen naked, but Jim tried to look away to be polite. That wasn't easy to do, because there were naked people in every direction.

"How long will it be before I am no longer uncomfortable bathing will all these people?"

"Oh, perhaps two days, perhaps three."

"I just realized that you've used the word 'perhaps' several times, rather than the word 'maybe'."

"I love the word perhaps. It is like saying a gentle breeze. Maybe is a strong word." They grinned. Jim forgot his embarrassment, and they walked back home.

Jim opened his backpack to get dry clothes to sleep in. He should have brought his dirty clothes to the river to wash, because he didn't have a clean set of dry clothes.

"Your clothes are still wet, Jim. They are the wrong clothes for this climate. You need silk like we wear. See, mine are already completely dry. You will need long pants and sleeves tonight to keep mosquitoes off you so you don't get malaria."

"I don't have any long pants or sleeves with me."

"Then, you must put this silk sheet over you. I will take you to the tailor tomorrow after I introduce you to the Priest and his teachers."

They settled down into their places on the bed, with Jim by the door, and then Tuc next to him. Nu and Aunt settled at the head of the bed, perpendicular to Tuc and Jim. Uncle brought the hibachi inside, with coals still in it, but banked.

"Why does Uncle bring the hot hibachi inside?"

"We need the smoke of the hibachi to keep mosquitoes out. It helps a little, and the lizards eat some mosquitoes. If you concentrate to completely relax, your body will cool." Jim rolled on his side, and concentrated on total relaxation.

Softly, Nu spoke, "Lila tov, Jim."

Nu

"What! You speak Hebrew too?"

Nu giggled. "My degree is in linguistics, Jim. Do you speak Hebrew?"

"Only a few words. Good night. Lila tov."

Lesson Plan

Jim stirred. He had to relieve himself. It was still dark out, with just a hint of the coming dawn. Could he go up to the flats? He swung his feet out of bed, and Nu stopped him. She pulled the metal chamber pot from under the bed. "Use this. If you go outside, you'll be shot. The police watch for anything that moves."

"Boker tov." Jim laughed. Nu had said goodnight in Hebrew, so he responded by saying good morning in Hebrew. Nu was grinning broadly. Jim eased himself onto the chamber pot so he wouldn't splash from a standing position.

Aunt boiled some water, and put some thin sheets in it for just a few seconds. She piled them on a plate, and set up breakfast, consisting of left over cold rice from the night before, and some julienne veggies that had been marinating somewhere over night. She spread several bowls of sauces on the bed.

"Jim, take rice paper like this, put some rice in it and some vegetables. Roll it up, and dip in one sauce at a time." Breakfast was easy to put together and easy to eat. It was good.

Nu

Walking to the market, Nu called one student, and sent him on an errand. He ran across the bridge to An Khe. "I asked him to see the Priest and try to get us an appointment later today. For now, we will meet with each workgroup and you can see how our school works."

"How many students do you have?"

"About six hundred. A little more, I think."

Jim's brow furrowed. "Where are they all? I only see a few small groups of children here."

"That is because they all do ....what would you call it, field work?"

"Yes, that would be good. Field work. Are they hard for you to find?"

"No. You will see."

A group of children had started following Nu and Jim. It grew. Nu spoke to them, and as more children joined the group she explained: "These children are my language students. They will follow us around, listen to us, and I invited them to ask questions. I want them to hear us speaking English, and to practice speaking with us in English. You will see soon why I teach a family of languages at once. I will also be teaching you as we teach them. Why don't you welcome them?"

Sheepish, Jim turned to the group. He wasn't sure what to say, but was about to see how Nu would tie this up in a neat package. "Welcome to class, kids! My name is Jim."

The group yelled out, "Hello, Sim!"

"It is Jim."

Nu interrupted, "There is no way to say the letter 'J', so it sounds closest to an 'S' to them. I have practiced to make a J. An English 'J' is made by a 'D' and a French 'J'."

Turning to the group, Nu asked, "Jim said 'Welcome'. What language group is that from?"

"German! Wilkommen!"

"Sehr gud! Notice how close sehr gud sounds to 'very good'. English belongs to two families of languages. Some English words come from the German family, and some come from the Latin family. What is 'welcome' in French?"

"Bienvenue!"

"Spanish?"

"Bienvenido."

"Italian?"

"Bienvenuto!"

Jim was smiling broadly. "Now I see why you teach a whole family of languages at once. They can draw parallels, and they reinforce what they've learned immediately!"

"Team, now we will teach Jim how to say hello in Vietnamese and in Chinese. I've told him that Vietnamese is a more formal language than Chinese. Show Jim how to say hello in Chinese."

The group said "Ni hao!"

Jim responded, "Knee how."

"Very good!" Nu took a stick and wrote 'Ni hao' in the dirt. She put a rising accent over 'Ni' and a 'u' shaped accent over 'hao'. "See, when we say 'Ni', our tone rises. When we say 'hao', our tone dips and comes back up. The accents tell us how to say the word."

"I see. That makes sense. How do you say hello in Vietnamese?"

"The same as in Italian: 'chao', but we spell it differently. Italian is 'ciao' and Vietnamese is 'chao'. But I told you that Vietnamese was more formal than Chinese. You use a title with hello in Vietnamese. If you are speaking to a young man you say, 'chao anh'. If you are speaking with an older or very important man, you say, 'chao ong'. If you are speaking with a young woman, it is 'chao co'. For an older woman, 'chao ba.' When you greet a child, say 'chao em.'"

"What is the difference between a girl child and a boy child?"

"No difference. 'Chao em'. We don't assign gender until they reach age where they can have children."

"I've noticed that spellings don't always match the sounds. Like the word for 'no', 'khong.' It sounds almost like 'calm.'"

"That is because you speak English. Our alphabet comes from the French. Before the French, we used the Chinese characters. The French gave us the western character set. The spellings come from how the French heard our language. You don't hear it the same as the French do. Some things you'll just have to accept."

"Damn the French."

Everyone laughed and relaxed. This was fun!

"Jim, the students are learning more than just English in this class. We are also teaching them how to teach. We need teachers, and some of the students may want to become teachers when they are adults. They will help me teach you. I also use older students to help teach younger students. Come, we will go to other work groups, and this group will help me show you what the other groups are doing."

The Most Important Job In Town

"The next group we will visit is working with the most important man in An Tuc. What do you think he does?"

"I have no idea. The mayor?"

"Nu laughed. We don't have a mayor or any kind of government here, but the most important man is our sluicemaster. He makes sure we have food to eat!"

"What is a sluicemaster?"

"He controls the water supply to our fields of rice. Rice must have just the right amount of water to grow and produce a lot of rice. The road we are walking on has other purposes. You see how the rice paddies have roads, dividing them?"

"Yes."

The roads are wide, to survive floods. They are also dams. We have trees on them that produce fruit. The tree roots hold the soil in place and make the dams strong. In between the trees, we have vegetables growing. The vegetables require less water than rice, so they are above the rice paddies. Watch your step as we cross here. This is called a sluice. It is a narrow opening between the upper paddie and lower paddie. Sluicemaster puts boards in the sluice to control how much water can flow through the sluice. He must watch it closely to control how good a crop of rice we will be able to harvest."

"Wow, there's a science to all this!"

They made their way down to a group of children who were talking with a very muddy old man. The man had only a few teeth, which didn't really line up in any fashion useful for chewing.

Jim silently reviewed the proper forms of greeting that he had just learned. As they approached the old man, Jim said, "Chao ong!"

The old man had already heard about Jim, and wanted to make a good impression, so he used the respectful form of greeting as well: "Chao ong! Lai xin." He held out his muddy hand and they shook hands with smiles.

Most of the hydrology students already spoke at least passable English, so they eagerly explained the principles of rice paddy hydrology, and managing sluice flow.

Sluicemaster spoke. "I have a test for you, Sim. This paddie is flooded. Water is flat across the paddie. Can you explain why water comes out the pipe at the other end, when this end of the pipe is under water in a flat paddy?"

Jim looked at the pipe. He could see that water was coming out the other end of the pipe. He also saw that water was flowing over the nearby sluice into the paddy. He thought a moment, and responded. "Yes. There is water coming in at this end to replace water that is being lost three ways. First, the rice is absorbing water to grow. Second, you have evaporation, so some water is being lost to the air. Third, some water is being absorbed into the soil in the underground aquifer. That aquifer is why you have wells to get drinking water. So the water that is flowing over this sluice is replacement water. It has to flow all the way to the other end of the paddie. Along the way, it has to pass many rows of growing rice. Each row of rice causes resistance to the flow, acting as a miniature sluice. Although the water appears to be even from one end of the paddy to the other, it really has a very slight slope. The pipe has much less resistance than the rice presents, so the water will come out of the pipe at the other end and form a head that is the real height of the water at this end."

"That is very good, Sim. Can you tell me how to use flowing water as a pump to pump water out of a paddie?"

"Yes. That is called the Venturi effect. If you pass water through a T valve, the flowing water will form a vacuum and pump water out of the perpendicular leg."

"Exactly. I would very much enjoy working with you and have you help explain these concepts. I have notebooks with formulas I have written, and would like you to review them."

"I would be very happy to work with you, Sluicemaster. You have the practical experience, and I have the theory from books. This will give me a wonderful laboratory to work with."

The sun was high in the sky, and it was getting intolerably hot. Nu suggested that they bathe before lunch and siesta. As they approached the market, the student that had gone to An Khe that morning came running over. "The priest say he would be happy to have you and Sim come for lunch tomorrow about fourteen o'clock."

Nu thanked him and turned to Jim. "That is good. We can have a short class tomorrow, then bathe before going to the French school. I have eaten with the priest before, and he serves French food with western utensils. He has his teachers eat with him, so you will get to meet them as well. He is a very formal man."

Jim was still muddy from being with the sluicemaster. They turned to the area of the river that is used for bathing, and got in, fully clothed. Washing their clothes first, they hung them to dry on shrubs at the river bank, and just soaked in the water for a while. The river was quite warm, and felt good.

"Nu, I have to tell you that when we first met, I thought you were only about nine or ten years old."

"Is it because I am very small?"

"Yes. Now that we have talked a lot, I know that you couldn't possibly be that age. I don't even think of you as a 'little girl' any more. I just think of you as 'Nu.'"

Nu

"Thank you, Jim. I was impressed with your knowledge of science. Science and math are not strong areas of study for me. I hope to learn these things from you. You are good at explaining these things."

"Thank you. I really like the way you teach language by teaching a family of languages at once. It is fun!"

They got out of the water, and were putting their clothes on, while chatting about different disciplines and how to effectively teach them. Jim was excited about Nu's teaching methods. Nu desperately hoped Jim would choose to work with her instead of the Catholic school.

"You don't have an erection today."

"Yes! My mind was on our conversation. I think I have that problem solved now. If I don't think about being naked, it won't embarrass me." Jim was pleased that Nu understood his predicament, and could speak so easily about it. Conversation would be easy with her.

The Priest

"We are supposed to meet the priest at fourteen o'clock, but my watch was stolen in Saigon. How will we know when it is fourteen?"

"We will guess with the sun. Time is not very important here. Almost nobody has a watch or even cares what time it is. Aunt will not make us lunch. Instead, we can take our bath and a short siesta so we are clean and rested when we meet the priest. After meeting with him, I will show you An Khe and where the American Army base is."

"That sounds good. I should go to the American base and let them know that I am here. I want to get some toothpaste too."

"Ooooo, that would be good. I would love to get toothpaste. We can get it in Saigon, but not here. I need a new toothbrush too. If you can find chocolate, that would be wonderful!"

Nu and Jim spent the morning visiting several more work groups, with the ever-present English students tagging along to use their English with Nu and Jim.

Nu

There were now about twenty students at any time, so Jim thought of them as "our entourage."

On the way to the bathing spot on the river, Jim stopped and asked, "Are these bananas?"

"Yes." Nu picked one, peeled it back, and took a bite. "They are good. Here's one that is ripe for eating."

"They don't look much like our bananas. They don't look very good. We wait until they turn yellow to eat them, but these are still green."

"I have seen your bananas. They look more like plantains, long and thin. We let them ripen before we eat them, and you can tell that they are ripe when they ooze brown fluid."

Jim peeled the banana and tasted it. It looked more like a large plum than a banana. It was messy to eat, and the brown ooze was sticky and sweet. The middle still tasted a bit green, but it was good. Looking around, Jim saw many fruits that he didn't recognize, and asked about them. One large tree had several oddly shaped fruits that were bigger than anything he had ever seen before. They were mostly green, with a rough exterior. They looked large enough to kill a man if they were to fall.

"What do you call this?"

"Jackfruit. I don't care for it, but you can eat it. It has very large seeds that you can roast in the hibachi, then smash them open with a stone. The seeds taste good, and are filling."

After washing their clothes and bathing, Nu and Jim went back home. Jim's clothes wouldn't be dry for a while, so he changed into a fresh pair of shorts and shirt. He had given up wearing socks, and now just wore sneakers on his bare feet, but he let the sneakers dry out in the sun while he rested. He wondered what the priest would be like. Nu hadn't said much about the other school or the priest.

On the way to the bridge, Nu pointed out a small fort about the size of a ranch house in America. It was lined in sand bags, and had sand bags on the roof. "This is the police station. They guard the bridge, and they guard the town at night."

"When you need them, how do you call them? I don't see a door."

"You call from outside and they come out. They live here, but it isn't a place you can go in. Just beyond, is the bunker where they guard the bridge."

Crossing the bridge, Jim noted that you could see police inside the bunker, smoking and taking life easy. The roof of the bunker gave them protection from the sun. It looked like they entered the bunker from below the bridge.

"This is An Khe. The first store is the bakery. Sometimes I stop here to purchase baguettes for breakfast instead of rice paper."

"The stores here are made of concrete rather than the mud and stick construction in An Tuc."

"Yes. This was a French town, and the buildings were built like in France, with concrete. I think they will last for hundreds of years. The American base is where the French had an airport."

"I can see the church ahead. It isn't far from where you live." Jim saw the school next door, and the courtyard between was enclosed with a concrete wall, with an iron gate. The gate was closed, but there was a doorway with an iron gate that was open. Children were playing in the courtyard. Jim saw that they were all wearing western style uniforms. The boys had khaki shorts and white shirts. The girls wore blue skirts and white shirts. Some were singing in French as they played. "They have their classes in French?"

"French and Vietnamese. The books are from French schools, so most lessons are in French." The bell rang, and children poured out of the school yard, to go home for lunch. "We are a little early, but that should not be a problem."

Walking up to the rectory, they were greeted by a Vietnamese woman who greeted them in French. "Bonjour! Comment allez-vous?" She led them into a waiting room with paintings of both religious scenes and French towns. They sat in wooden chairs, awaiting the priest. The woman who greeted them brought tea in decorative china, with bowls of lemon slices, sugar, and a decanter with milk. Quietly, Jim said, "It is just like we stepped from Vietnam into France." Nu smiled. Jim could see she was uncomfortable.

The priest came into the room, extended his hand

first to Jim, then to Nu. They exchanged greetings in French. Jim's French was not good, so Nu translated his responses. The priest led them into the formal dining room, where five Vietnamese women were just taking their seats. The priest motioned for Jim to sit opposite him at the table. After all were seated, the priest said grace in French. There was already a basket of baguettes and a bowl of butter on the table. The table was set in French formal, with a soup spoon at each place, perpendicular to the other utensils. It would be used first. The priest asked in French what Jim was doing in Vietnam, and what he hoped to accomplish. Jim had difficulty answering in French, so Nu was translating.

A taller, very thin woman, obviously pregnant, came in with a tray of soup. Nu greeted her in Mandarin. Jim was glad to have the opportunity to practice his Chinese. The woman put bowls of soup in front of everyone, and greeted Jim in English. Jim responded in Mandarin: "Wo hen hao, xie-xie, ni na?"

The woman beamed, and answered, "Xie-xie! Wo hen hao!"

Jim tasted the soup. It was refrigerator-cold, and appeared to be a potato soup with leek and watercress, with a hint of ginger. It was very tasty, and refreshingly cold. He asked what it was, and the priest said it was vichyssoise.

As they finished their soup, the Chinese woman gathered the bowls and delivered plates of steak, au jus, with fresh asparagus. The steak was the best that Jim had ever had. Jim turned to the priest and complimented him on the steaks. The priest responded, "Il etat Chateaubriand."

"You must have a refrigerator."

Nu broke in: "Yes, the church has a generator, and some large refrigerators and freezers. The priest brought the Chinese family from Saigon to cook for the school, so he supplies everything. To make extra money, the Chinese family has a restaurant next door where they cook this. Many American soldiers eat there."

The priest's schoolteachers didn't speak much, but did ask questions, in French. They wanted to know how Jim expected to teach if his French was so poor. They obviously didn't like the idea of Jim joining them, and the tension was high. Jim saw that Nu was very uncomfortable. He would solve that straightaway.

"I was wondering the same thing. I don't think I would be a good fit here. Nu needs help with engineering, science and math. I would be a good fit with her."

Nu had trouble concealing her delight as she translated. Everyone relaxed, and the color came back into Nu's face. That settled, the rest of lunch went very well, and Jim offered to help the teachers with math, science and engineering if they wished.

After bidding everyone goodbye, Jim and Nu left the compound. Jim noticed a shiny Mercedes town car in a carport next to the rectory. The priest lived very well indeed.

When they couldn't be seen by the priest, Nu did

a delighted little jig that resembled the Irish clogging dance. Jim thought she looked like a skeleton hanging on strings that were being jiggled. They both laughed until tears ran down their cheeks. "You make me very happy today, Jim! What do you think of the priest?"

"I think he is an arrogant snob!"

Rose

"Since we are already in An Khe, I will take you through and show you what is here. Next to the school is the restaurant that cooked our lunch. You can usually get Chateaubriand here." They continued walking. Passing a trinket shop, Nu pointed out a pair of shower clogs. "You should get these. You are wet when you put your sneakers on." Jim agreed, and bought the clogs. Most of the people in town wore clogs or walked barefoot. Clogs were very practical.

"Many steambaths and massage parlors for the soldiers."

"I think they get more than a bath or massage."

"Yes."

"This is the road to the Army base."

Jim looked down the straight road. He could see the gate and guardshack about four hundred metres away. It was open space all the way to the gate, for security. The base looked very large, with concertina wire stretching as far as the eye could see to the left and right.

"There is nothing farther. We can turn around. Oh! I want you to meet my friend, Rose." They crossed the street, and up to a smiling young woman sitting in front of a cement building. "Hello, Rose! I want you to meet my friend, Jim."

"Hello, Jim, I'm pleased to meet you!"

"Chao co, minh oi?"

Rose laughed, "Nu is teaching you well!"

"Rose is my friend from Saigon. She is a singer, and has made a few popular records."

Rose wasn't made up like other Vietnamese girls. Her hair was short, and had some curl. She wore a little makeup, and western clothes, including a knit blouse. Jim thought she might be half French. "Rose is a western name. Do you have a Vietnamese name?"

"Yes, but Rose is my stage name, and that's what I prefer to use."

"Can you earn a living as a singer in An Khe?"

"Oh no, Saigon was too dangerous, so I came here. I am working as a prostitute. I hope to make enough money to get my own band by the end of the war. Would you like to hear me sing?"

"Yes I would."

Rose went inside and got a guitar and two more chairs. They sat facing one-another, and she started singing a Vietnamese love song. Vietnamese is a very tonal language, more so than Chinese, and it was the prettiest singing that Jim ever heard. Nu was smiling broadly, thoroughly enjoying the music. Jim had never heard a voice capable of changing tones so quickly. "Will you sing for us, Jim?" She offered the guitar to Jim, who first played "Grandfather's Clock" without singing. Jim was a finger-picker, not a strummer. When he had the feel for the frets on this guitar, he sang "Love Me Tender" and the French song, "Plasir d'Amour." His booming bass voice brought several neighbors over to listen.

"Vietnamese men don't have deep voices like yours, I love it! You are welcome to come sing with me any time you want."

"I'd like that very much."

Nu suggested that they both sing at the Tet new year's festival in February. They then headed back home to tell Aunt and Uncle that Jim would be working with Nu rather than at the French school. Along the way, Nu pointed out different businesses, and they talked easily.

"There were many things I wanted to tell you about the French school, but I didn't want to influence you. I wanted you to see for yourself. Tell me your thoughts."

"After hearing the teachers explain the curriculum, I think that they are teaching the children how to be servants to the French. The priest doesn't seem to know that the French are gone."

"Exactly. I teach practical things that are appropriate to Vietnam's economy and to the future I hope we will have. I want us to be ready to join the world economy.

I want to turn out business people and engineers and inventors. I don't want them to be servants."

"I agree completely." Jim went silent, lost in thought.

"What is wrong, Jim?"

"I was thinking about American schools." He paused, stopping in the roadway. "Thinking about what American schools teach, I think they go wrong in the same way as the priest's school. American schools teach the subjects and discipline necessary for the students to get jobs. I think they should teach the students to make jobs, not to get jobs."

"Jim, did you just now think of this, or did you know it before today?"

"I knew something was wrong with our schools, but I wasn't sure what it was until I saw the futility of the French school."

Crossing the bridge, the kids immediately joined them to find out how the interview with the priest went. They were excited when they found out that Jim decided to work with Nu rather than at the Catholic school.

"After we tell Aunt and Uncle, I will take you to meet our tailor so you can get some practical clothes."

Kim

"Hello, Kim! I would like you to meet a new teacher, Jim. He is from America."

Jim looked at this man, who was much taller than the Vietnamese. He had been eating from a bowl of rice and a bowl of stronger smelling veggies, which he put down to offer his hand.

"Welcome, Jim! We are pleased to have you here. I've already heard about you. Would you like to have some kim-chee and rice?"

"Thank you, we've already eaten, but that smells interesting, so I'd like to try it." Nu accepted also. Kim gave each a small bowl of rice and put several bowls of kim-chee on the table.

"These are three of the kinds of kim-chee that I make. Some are made very hot, some very salty and some with various spices like garlic. Kim-chee is fermented cabbage, but you can flavor it any way you like. I make my own right here."

Jim noticed that Kim's English had a decided British accent. "You are Korean?"

"Yes. My family escaped North Korea when I was small, and lived in Seoul. I came to Vietnam a few years ago, and moved to the mountains for the climate. This is wonderful! It is not humid here, and there is no winter."

"Nu says that I need some practical clothes for this climate."

"Your clothes won't dry well. I will make you silk pants and shirts that will protect you from mosquitoes and will dry quickly."

"Isn't the black silk very hot in the sun?"

"The silk gets hot, but air blows right through it, so you will feel cool. You are about my size, so it will be easy to make. The pants will cost 800 dong, and the shirts will be 500. How many of each will you need?"

"Two of each will be good for now."

"Come back tomorrow afternoon, and they will be ready."

Jim and Nu thanked Kim for the kim-chee, and went home.

Letters Home

"I want to try to send a letter home to let my family know where I am. Do you write your father?"

"Yes. There is no post here, so I have to go to Qui Nhon to post letters. They have telephones there too, but they are not good. I have some letters that I have written to my father, but haven't yet sent. If you go to the American base, would you see if they will send them to Saigon?"

"Yes. I'll go tomorrow."

"Then I'll write another letter now to my father, and you can take these with you."

After lunch the next day, Jim took Nu's letters, and drove the motorcycle to the American base at An Khe. It was only a ten minute ride on the motorcycle, and the breeze felt good as he rode. As he approached the main gate of the base, the M. P. motioned for him to park the motorcycle outside the base. "You can come in, Sir, but you have to leave your bike outside."

"Thanks. Is there someplace where I can mail letters home?"

"The post office is straight ahead. Keep going, and bear right to the mess hall. When you get there, take a right, and there is a sign on the post office. You'll see a line of barracks there."

"Thank you."

Parking the motorcycle, Jim walked through the gate. The motor pool was on the left, and there were large oil tanks on the right. Jim took note of the signs on various buildings. The roads were not paved, and had been oiled to keep the dust down. He saw a sign saying, "Welcome to Camp Radcliffe, home of the 173d Airborne Brigade and First Cavalry, Air Mobile." Farther ahead, he saw a billboard for A&W Root beer. It had the familiar frosted mugs, but at the bottom of the billboard it read, "Next A&W 11,000 miles straight ahead." Someone had a good sense of humor!

After twenty minutes of walking, he saw the mess hall, and turned right. There was the post office. Walking in, he found a soldier at the counter. He explained that he was teaching school in the next town, and wanted to mail some letters, and set up a way to receive mail. The clerk explained that soldiers could just write "Free" on their letters, but that he would have to buy stamps. No problem. Receiving mail was another matter. He could rent a post office box for $1 a month. He found out what return address he would need to use. He rented the box, and went outside to add this information to his letters, and to put the return address on his envelopes. The return address would be "Jim Flannery, An Tuc School, C/O Hq Co., 173d Airborne Brigade, APO S.F. 96250."

After sealing the envelopes, he went back in, purchased stamps, and asked about mailing Nu's letters to her father. "I'm sorry, Sir. Mail goes straight to San Francisco. We don't interface with the Vietnamese post office." Jim thanked him, and asked if there was a P. X. where he could get some toothpaste. The clerk gave him directions, and Jim left.

Turning past the mess hall, Jim saw a building with a sign indicating they had pizza. Across the street, there was an open-air theater with benches that could seat a few hundred people. Turning left, he passed many buildings with signs he didn't recognize. Looking up, there was a mountain with radio towers. Jim noticed that the mountain had a concertina wire fence at both the bottom and the top of the mountain. He thought that was odd.

One building he passed had the Signal Corps insignia, and a sign that read "An Khe M.A.R.S. Station." Good! Maybe he could get a phone patch and call home. He stopped in. They said they'd be glad to try to get him a phone patch, but soldiers would always come first. That was appropriate. "What is the best time to try?"

"Dusk and dawn. The signals follow the gray line around the earth, when the ionosphere is charged." That would be difficult with the curfew, but he'd try some time.

Another 10 minutes walk brought him to the P. X. He tried to enter, but was turned away. "You need to be in uniform or have a military I.D. card to enter." So much for toothpaste.

Lt. Col. Anthony Herbert

Retracing his steps back toward the gate, Jim passed the theater, and saw a small shelter with screens. "Officer's Latrine." It was the first loo he had passed, and he needed to relieve himself. Inside, he found a single long bench with 5 holes. Each had a toilet seat. There were also newspapers to read. He sat on a relatively clean toilet seat, and started going through the newspapers. He hadn't heard any news in a week, and was anxious to find out what was happening.

Hearing the screen door slam, Jim looked up and saw a mountain of a man come in and grab another toilet seat.

"Civilian?"

"Yes. I'm a school teacher in An Tuc. Jim Flannery."

"Tony Herbert. I'm the Inspector General."

"What does an Inspector General do, Tony?"

"We investigate things. We're not terribly popular, because we go right through red tape, and cause a lot of trouble for people who have done things wrong." Tony grinned. "That's okay with me. Being popular has never been important to me."

"Sounds like you enjoy the distinction. Hey, I just got a post office box here, and I should probably check in somewhere just so the Army knows I'm here. Would that be the Provost Marshal?"

"Yes. Come across the street to my office, and I'll take you over to see the Provost."

Tony's office looked pretty nice. There was a wall of filing cabinets, all locked. The furniture was standard government issue, but there were lots of chairs, coffee table, and two large desks. "This is my right-hand man, Sgt. Major John Bittorie."

"Hello, John. I'm Jim Flannery. I'm a school teacher in An Tuc."

"Hello Sir! G..g..g..good to meet you." The Sgt Major had a serious stuttering problem, but spoke with a strong, authoritative voice. The three spoke for a while and got acquainted.

"I just set up a post office box, and tried to buy toothpaste at the P. X., but they won't let me in."

"I think we can fix that, Jim."

"Sgt. Major, fire up the jeep. We'll introduce Jim to the Provost Marshal, then take him to the P. X. for his toothpaste."

"Yes Sir!"

At the Provost's office, Jim filled out a contact card, presented his passport, and explained what he was doing in An Tuc. Leaving, Col. Herbert told the Sgt. Major to give Jim a tour of the base. They turned onto the perimeter road, which had guard towers all along it, spaced so that there was no distance out of sight of a guard tower.

"This is a very large base. The perimeter is eighteen miles."

The Sgt. Major went on to tell his boss' story. "The Colonel was an enlisted man in the Korean War. He worked his way up to Sgt. Major. He was the most highly decorated man in Korea, and received a battlefield commission. After Korea, he went on to get degrees in psychology and law." The Sgt. Major was obviously impressed with his boss and loved to tell his story.

"I saw a mountain inside the base with concertina at the bottom and top. What's with that?"

"That's Hong Kong Mountain. Our communications are at the top, but the mountain isn't secure. Sometimes Charlie shoots at us from the mountain, so we have a guarded perimeter at the bottom and the top. We think that Charlie has a tunnel to it from somewhere. Monkeys wearing backpacks have been shot crossing the perimeter."

"You're kidding! Monkeys?"

"Not kidding. It is official."

"This is the airport. It was an old French landing field, so when the Army found it, they just built the base around it. That's the terminal and weather station."

The terminal was like a French Provincial house, with real windows, screened.

"You should be able to catch a flight to anywhere from here, if there's a spare seat."

Turning, they went back to the P. X. The Colonel asked for the commanding officer of the P. X. "Lieutenant, this is Jim Flannery. He will never have identification when he comes here. He can't tell you what unit he is with, and you can't ask."

"Yes Sir!"

"Get what you need, Jim."

Jim picked up a couple of tubes of Colgate, toothbrushes, and a few tins of tuna. They left, and headed toward the main gate. "Sgt. Major, stop at the quartermaster."

"Yes, Sir!"

"Jim, if you need a canteen or anything, this is where to get it." They went in, and Jim saw rows and rows of uniforms, canteens, green cans of coffee, knives and other issue items. He picked out a knife, web belt and canteen. Colonel Herbert gave the quartermaster the same instructions that he had given at the P. X. The Sgt. Major then drove Jim out the gate to his motorcycle.

"Any time you're in the area, stop in and pay us a visit. I'd like to hear more about your adventures in An Tuc."

"Thanks Tony, John. I'll look forward to it!"

Traveling Gifts

Arriving back home, Jim handed Aunt the tins of tuna. Though she didn't read English, she saw the fish on the label, and was clearly thrilled to have fish to serve at the next meal. He then gave Nu and Tuc new toothbrushes and toothpaste. "What is in the big tin, Jim?"

"Café."

"Ooooooo. That will be good tomorrow morning. I'll get us some drippers at the market, and some sugar. When you travel, bring some tins of tuna with you to give as gifts. People will appreciate it."

Jim handed Nu the letters that he wasn't able to post. "I was able to set up mail for myself, but they said that the mail goes straight to America, and doesn't connect with the Vietnamese post office."

"That is no problem. We should go to Qui Nhon soon, and I will try to ring up my father from the post office. There are many things for me to show you along the way."

Getting Acclimated

The next two weeks were quiet, as Nu took Jim with her to work with all the workgroups. The language students tagged along at all times, so they always had a crowd that had grown to about thirty children. There were always questions about America. The students were fascinated with stories of America. They were anxious to get electricity, so they could have things like refrigerators, electric lights and fans. The possibilities that refrigeration alone could provide, captivated them. Just imagine being able to store food for weeks!

There was never a problem with discipline. The Vietnamese culture was such that nobody would consider getting into any trouble. They knew that they were behind the rest of the world in technology and lifestyle, and they wanted desperately to catch up. They were eager to learn everything. Banking and investing were of particular interest. There was no bank in An Tuc. People just kept whatever little money they had at home. All transactions were in cash. Jim explained how people in America would invest in new products to bring them to market. "When someone comes up with a good idea, but doesn't have the money to build a factory to produce things, he presents his idea to the marketplace, and if he can convince people that his idea is a good one, people will lend him money to get started. He then pays dividends to the people who invested to get him started. As the company grows, the stock becomes more valuable, and all the people who own shares in the company are rewarded for their investment." This was a new concept to the children and most of the adults.

Bee Hives and
Stone Age People

Nu and Jim had gotten into the habit of exploring after siesta and before dinner. Often, they would take the motorcycle, so they could go farther. A short distance out of town, and not far past the road to the American base, Jim stopped, and pointed to some small mud buildings shaped like bee hives or igloos. "What are those buildings? I have seen them many times.

"That is where we make charcoal for cooking. Wood is put along the walls, and a fire is lit in the centre. The heat dries the wood, and makes it clean for cooking. If you go farther, you will see the forest come almost to the road. That is where the wood is gathered."

They drove ahead a couple more kilometers, and were higher in altitude. There were rough roads into the forest. Several small, two-wheeled carts were by the forest, with tee-yokes. "It is downhill from here to the charcoal kilns, so it is easy for the men to carry the wood."

Driving farther, they came to a village that was much

different than An Tuc. Nu had Jim stop outside the village. "This is a Montagnard village."

"The French word for mountaineer."

"Yes. These people are not farmers. They do not grow rice or vegetables. Instead, they move from place to place, hunt animals and gather up what food they can find. They do not understand money or property, and just take what they want. They have only a simple language. They do not mix with Vietnam people."

Instead of mud and stick buildings, their shelters were only stick, and were built off the ground on stilts. Even the adults were completely naked. They were short like Vietnamese, but much heavier, and darker-skinned. "Are they racially the same as Vietnamese?"

"No. Like us, they do not have a fold on their eyelid, but my father says they are closer to white people than to any Asian. They are an ancient people that migrate from country to country and do not recognize any borders."

Nu and Jim walked into the camp, and Nu conversed briefly with some of the people in a strange tongue. They didn't mind having visitors, but weren't excited about it either. Jim noticed that while they were all completely naked, many of them wore quivers over their shoulders, and carried small crossbows. He also saw some spears and stone knives. The people were very dark skinned. He looked at their eyes, and saw the lack of a fold in the upper eyelid that Nu had mentioned. The rest of the facial features were more like westerners than Asians. They looked like powerful, healthy people.

Nu

Heading back home, Jim said, "We should plan a trip to Qui Nhon so you can mail your letters. Would you like to go tomorrow?"

"Tomorrow is Saturday. The government post will be closed after lunch and all day Sunday, so we should wait until Monday. I will write another letter during siesta tomorrow. Along the way, I want to show you many things. We will need a full day.

Qui Nhon

Monday morning, Nu shook Jim awake early. They had decided to wear western clothes to Qui Nhon. Nu pulled a box from under the bed, and took out a pair of shorts and white blouse. They changed into western clothes, quickly ate breakfast, and headed out as soon as curfew was over. It was refreshingly cool to ride the motorcycle at dawn. The street was deserted as they headed out of town.

When they got to the tents at the top of An Khe Pass, they stopped at the tents, as the first aid girls were just setting up for the day. Nu spoke with them briefly, then turned to Jim. "On the way down the pass, I will point out where we will stop on the way back to collect champignons. What is that in English?"

"Mushrooms."

"Yes, mushrooms. It is my favorite place! After we are in the valley, you will see tents on the left. That is the Kiwi Red Cross hospital. We can stop there too. They are very nice doctors. Sometimes they come to An Tuc to help sick or injured people. You will like them."

Nu

Nu pointed out the stone temple that Jim had noticed on his way to An Khe. "We will stop here also on the way back. It is Cao Dai. Very interesting." Jim nodded yes.

It was downhill all the way to Qui Nhon, and they made good time. Entering the city, Nu pointed the way to the post office. Once inside, she posted her letters, and asked for the box for An Tuc and An Khe. There were about two hundred letters in the box, and Nu picked out a dozen. "Put these in your backpack to bring back. I will deliver them when we get home. One letter is for Rose."

Nu slipped into a telephone booth, and picked up the receiver. She asked for Saigon. It was not long, and she asked for her father's home number. No answer. She then asked for the hospital. Her father was in surgery. She left a message for him that she had mailed letters.

Leaving the post office, Nu took Jim on a tour of the city, pointing out local landmarks of interest. When they got to the American base, Jim pulled in and asked where the Red Cross office was. The guard wouldn't let them in, but offered to call. Jim asked for Nora Hadley. She answered, and came to pick them up in her jeep.

"It is too early for lunch, but let me give you a tour of the hospital, then will you join me for lunch?" They agreed.

Once at the hospital, Jim made the introductions. Nora thanked him for stopping by to bring her up to date, and to introduce Nu. Nora proudly showed off the modern hospital, answering Nu's questions. Nu explained that her father is a doctor at the government hospital in Saigon, so she was very interested in the differences between the Vietnamese and American hospitals. Nora couldn't answer all the questions, but asked nurses as they walked along.

At eleven o'clock, Nora took them to the cafeteria. There, she had many questions for Nu about how she runs the school. Nora was very interested in the workgroup concept. Jim volunteered that they had interviewed with the Priest, but thought all he was doing was training a new generation of servants for the French.

Cao Dai

After leaving the hospital, they headed back toward An Tuc. In an hour, they reached the Cao Dai temple, and parked the bike nearby. "You will find this interesting. Cao Dai is not a religion. It is a place for all religions to go. They have many religious students that go there to research the similarities between the religions. I like it. They say, the stories are the same, the lessons are the same. The names and places may be different, but they all tell the same story."

Jim opened the door for Nu, and they stepped in. Adjusting for the lesser light, Jim suddenly gasped in horror.

"Jim! What is wrong?"

"That swastika!" It was like he had suddenly stepped into Nazi Germany.

"That is Buddhist symbol. See the eight corners, for the eight right thoughts?"

"How long have the Buddhists used that symbol?"

"Thousands of years."

Jim relaxed a little, but could still feel his spine tingling. He accepted Nu's explanation, and filled her in on how the symbol had been used in recent years. Nu said that the Buddhists also use a wheel with eight spokes.

Nu took Jim around the temple, stopping at each section. There were a few people reading at tables. The sections reminded Jim of the Catholic "Stations Of The Cross." There were sections for Christian, Jewish, Moslem, Buddhist, Shinto, Hindu and others. Jim had trouble taking his eyes off the swastika. He shuddered every time he saw it.

Kiwis

Back out on the road, they headed toward their next stop, the New Zealand Red Cross hospital. When they reached it, there were some American Army jeeps parked outside. Parking near them, they headed toward the smaller tent that was the office.

"Hello, Geoff! Hello, Neville!"

"G'day, Nu! Good to see you! Who is your friend?"

Nu made the introductions, and Geoff introduced a team of American civilian doctors. "These doctors are forensic pathologists. They are touring American military hospitals, doing autopsies. They stopped here to compare notes with us."

Nu and Jim looked at one-another, perplexed. "Why do autopsies here, and why civilian doctors?"

An American doctor explained, "This is one place where we can get young American men that have been killed in battle, not as a result of illness. We are studying cardio-vascular disease. What we are learning is that the majority of the population has hearts and blood vessels that already show significant coronary artery disease. It is our American diet. We have also done autopsies on Vietnamese, and find that old Vietnamese people have better hearts than young Americans. Heart disease is almost unheard of in Asia. It is strokes that kill Asians."

Nu chimed in, "That is accurate. My father is a doctor in the government hospital in Saigon. He has told me the same thing. We have a lot of salt in our diet, which contributes to strokes. We have almost no meat. The people on the coast eat a lot of fish." Nu asked for paper, and wrote her father's name and contact information. "My father speaks English, and would be glad to talk with you. He would also like to know that you spoke with me. Please visit him in Saigon and tell him that I miss him very much." The doctors agreed.

Since the Kiwis were busy with the American doctors, Jim and Nu simply thanked them and promised to return soon to visit.

Champignons

It was slow going up the lacettes with the weight of two people and the baggage they had collected along the way. Jim asked Nu to tell him where to turn for the mushrooms. He turned down an almost invisible trail that Nu pointed out. "Stop here!" Jim stopped, and they hid the bike in shrubbery. "It is perhaps twenty minutes to the mushrooms. Is that one word or two?"

"One word."

"That makes more sense. There is a wonderful waterfall by the mushrooms. It feels so good! This is one of my very favorite places in the world!"

As they walked, they could feel the air getting more humid. Pretty soon, they felt spray on their faces, and could hear the thunder of waterfalls just ahead. "We should leave our clothes here so they don't get wet. We will shower, collect mushrooms and ginger root, then come back for our clothes." They left their clothes lying in the sun on a rock, and picked their way to the waterfalls. Nu stepped under the falling water, and smiled broadly. Jim joined her. They just stood there for ten minutes feeling the cool water falling on their heads.

It was heavenly. Both were laughing and grinning when they stepped out. Nu had brought some plastic bags to collect the mushrooms and ginger root. She showed Jim which mushrooms to collect. Pretty soon, they had a full bag of mushrooms. "We need your knife to dig the ginger." They went back to where their clothes were, and got the knife. Jim thought that they must look pretty silly, naked, picking mushrooms by a waterfall. He no longer felt uncomfortable being naked. "Leave your clothes here. We will get muddy getting the ginger root, and can wash the mud off ourselves and the roots before we come back."

Drying Mushrooms

It was almost dinner when they got back home. Aunt quickly prepared dinner, as Nu spread the mushrooms out on a large silk cloth in the sun, just outside the door. Tuc would guard the mushrooms to keep the neighborhood dogs from stealing them. She dumped out the ginger root as well, and said that when it was dry, she would put the ginger in an open box under the bed. "How do you store ginger without refrigeration?"

"You should never refrigerate ginger. It will go bad quickly. It should be stored only in a dry place. The mushrooms need to dry. They won't dry enough before sundown, so we will spread them again in the morning, and let the sun dry them thoroughly." They changed into their silk clothes, ate dinner, and went for their bath before bed. It had been a long day, but a lot of fun. They would sleep soundly that night. "I am sorry my father wasn't available to talk with you today. I wanted you to meet him. Thank you for introducing me to Nora." Nu gathered up the mushrooms for the night, and put them away safely. "We will wait until the sun is strong before putting them out to dry tomorrow. These mushrooms won't be good until they've dried thoroughly."

A Surprise Wakeup

A week passed. Monday morning, Nu touched Jim awake. "Merry Christmas!"

"Huh?"

"Joyeaux Noel. Froliche Weinachten. It is Christmas day!"

"How can that be, it is still summer? Oh, I get it. It isn't summer, it is just hot. It doesn't feel like Christmas when it is hot. Well, Merry Christmas to you too!" They laughed. Would there be class today? No, Nu had given the students the day off in case Jim wanted to go to church.

"We can go to church today if you'd like. Are you Catholic?"

"Not really, but I would go with you."

Nu got out her western shorts and blouse, so Jim put on his shorts. They walked up to the French church, and waited until the doors opened. There were about two hundred Vietnamese, and perhaps thirty American soldiers. Mass was very long, and in French. Jim kept dozing off, and Nu would prop him up. Jim wasn't the only one dozing. There was a small choir, and Jim was surprised to see Rose singing in the choir. Jim wondered whether the priest knew that Rose was a prostitute. Jim let his mind wander to stay awake. His derriere hurt from the hard pew, and he squirmed.

After Mass, the priest exited first, to shake hands and wish everyone a merry Christmas. "I'm glad to see you again, Jim. I was hoping to see you more often."

"Merci, mon Pere." Jim left it at that –just polite. He really didn't like this man.

Jim and Nu waited for Rose, and chatted for a few minutes. Jim agreed to meet with Rose in the afternoons and practice some songs to sing at the Tet festival.

Walking home, Nu asked Jim, "You had trouble staying awake. Was it the priest?"

"He is a windbag."

"What is windbag?"

"He talks and talks and talks and talks."

"Ha ha, I understand windbag now."

"Do you suppose the priest knows that Rose is a prostitute?"

"Would it matter? A person's work doesn't make someone bad. Prostitution is not bad in Vietnam, or in France. She could even be serving the priest's needs."

Preparation For Tet Festival

Jim was working with a group in the market place. As they discussed commerce, a student asked to borrow Jim's knife. Handing it to her, Jim saw her peel and slice a long, irregularly shaped root vegetable. "What is that?"

"This is coulan. Here, taste." She handed Jim a slice. It tasted like a raw yam or sweet potato. "You can eat raw, or boil or put in charcoal. Is good?"

"I'll try it cooked." It gave Jim an idea. He wanted to prepare something to give out at the Tet festival. There would be lots of visiting, and lots of special foods cooked only for this biggest holiday of Asian life. Jim sniffed various spices from the vendors as he moved through the market. Over time, he located what appeared to be what he would need: summer savory, marjoram, and cayenne. He would try a small batch of two old family recipes to see if these ingredients would work. He brought some coulan home, and boiled one piece, while baking the other in the charcoal. Coulan was much better cooked. It was very similar to yam.

Nu

The next day, Jim got some more coulan, onion, savory, marjoram and cayenne. He explained to Aunt what he was doing. The recipes he wanted to make were French Canadian stuffings. Usually made with mashed potato, he hoped the coulan would be an adequate substitute. Coulan proved too sweet for one recipe that called for savory and onion, so Jim tried the other.

Making a batch of mashed coulan was easy. Jim added ground marjoram, and cayenne. Not sweet enough. Jim added sugar. That was very good! The Canadian recipe called for bacon, but where could he get some? Perhaps at the American base.

When he went to get his mail, he went to the quartermaster and asked if bacon was available. Yes, it came in green cans! He picked up a can, and planned his festival offering. Without using the bacon, Jim made a batch of the stuffing. Nu, Tuc, Aunt and Uncle all loved the recipe and thought it would be a wonderful offering at Tet. The can of bacon was as large as a coffee can, and would make a lot of the stuffing. That would be okay, since there would be a lot of people to serve!

Practice

Jim had to wait a little while for Rose to finish with a client, so he went to the Chinese restaurant, next to the church. He had a cup of the wonderful Vietnamese coffee. As he sat, he wondered whether the priest would be going to the Tet festival.

Rose welcomed Jim and suggested that they sit out back in the shade. She brought her guitar, and some paper to keep notes. Jim asked, "Do you suppose the priest will come to the festival?"

"Yes! He will bring his teachers, too. They travel as a group. They are also in the choir, so they might sing along with us."

"Then, we should sing things that they know. Do you know 'Dominique' or 'Plasir D'Amour?'"

"I love 'Dominique!' I heard you sing 'Plasir D'Amour', and it sounded easy to learn. We could do a duet, and invite the teachers to join in. What else do you have in mind?"

"I was thinking about 'Love Me Tender' and 'Sixteen tons.'"

"Good! Your bass voice will sound good with those songs. I was thinking that it would be difficult for you to learn any Vietnamese songs, but you could be our drums like in an a cappella group. You wouldn't need to know any words, just keep the beat. Listen, I'll sing a song and then I'll sing a bass line so you can see what I mean."

Rose had a large repertoire of songs. Most were Vietnamese but she also knew popular French and English songs. Over the next few weeks, they worked out how they wanted to do the show. The festival would last a whole week, but there was no electricity, so there was no sound system. They would be able to sing the same songs over and over, with the audience changing over the week.

Arrangements had been made with the police so they could have the festival into the evening without worrying about the curfew. Jim also visited with the Provost Marshal, so he would know there would be after hours festivities.

The Day Before

There were a lot of preparations for Tet. It was the only national holiday, and everyone looked forward to it every year. People stocked up on food to prepare. There would be chicken and rabbit and duck served to visitors. Normally, these things weren't in the diet, but this was a celebration! Almost everyone would be in their doorways, or wandering around town celebrating and renewing old friendships.

Jim noticed a lot of Vietnamese soldiers in town. They were coming home for the celebration. At Tet, everything would stop, and the country would be one huge celebration. Typically, the soldiers would be allowed to go on leave for the week, and there would be only a skeleton crew at each base.

Jim had collected enough coulan, marjoram, sugar and cayenne to make his stuffing. How to cook the bacon would be a problem. He had gone to the mess hall at An Khe to see how they cooked a whole can of bacon at a time, and they showed him that they used a French fryer. He didn't have one. Nu suggested that he cook it right in the can. He would try.

Nu

At siesta, Jim went over his notes of the songs that he planned to sing with Rose. Silently, he practiced in his mind. They wouldn't start to sing until sundown, because it would be just too hot until the sun set.

Tet, 1968

Truong Nhu Tang had sent couriers throughout the country, each carrying large sacks of Piasters, the Vietnamese currency. Some had left as much as six weeks before. As far as anyone knew, this was just a normal payroll for the Viet Cong troops in all corners of the country. A few couriers had been captured, as always. He was right on top of the problem, and dispatched fresh couriers with more money. Tang was the Justice Minister for the Viet Cong. Coming from a wealthy family, his father wanted him to become a pharmacist, but he rebelled, and decided to become a banker. Now he was the top banker for the Viet Cong government, a shadow government that hoped to take over Vietnam. He was young, and energetic. As a top official, he knew of the plans for what would become known as the "Tet Offensive." Only senior officers and officials knew the plan, and only a very few knew that it would be carried out across the entire country as a whole, and would coincide with the Tet holiday.

Tang was not Communist. Although the Viet Cong received supplies from the Communists of North Vietnam, there were very few Viet Cong that subscribed to Communism. As a banker, Tang was a pure Capitalist. He just wanted to remove an ever changing and totally corrupt Saigon government. Saigon changed its leaders as often as some people changed their underwear. Every new despot seemed more ugly than the last. Tang was committed to reform. He considered himself a Nationalist. Though the North Vietnamese had promised they would not ask for anything after the war, Tang had a nagging fear that they would take over.

The Viet Cong had taken heavy casualties, and were very discouraged. Many had deserted to take advantage of the "Chieu Hoi" amnesty plan. If they didn't move soon, the war would be over. The master plan for Tet would be to wait until the South Vietnamese soldiers were mostly off on holiday leave, then to do the unexpected: march right into the major cities, seize them and hold them. Local cadre had a basic understanding of their own small pieces of the puzzle without knowing the full extent.

Some Viet Cong soldiers were homesick, and wanted to go home for the holiday. A few had captured South Vietnamese Army uniforms. They could slip away quietly, and join the large throng of real South Vietnamese soldiers, and just go home. Some of those even quietly planned to join the Chieu Hoi Amnesty after the holiday.

Nguyen Thi Tho

Tho hated Pleiku. The red dust got into everything. The valley stretched for a couple hundred kilometers north and south, and fifty east to west. Agent orange had killed all the greenery. U S Army track vehicles plied the valley all day long, grinding the red clay soil into ever finer dust. Many of the residents of the city had left the area. This area was strategically important to the Viet Cong because it was the only feasible travel route along the western border with Cambodia and Laos. Tho was the local Viet Cong paymaster. A courier had just dropped off a large sack of Piasters with her. It was her duty to bring it to the local cadres. Over the next few days, she took smaller packets of money, strapped to her belly to make her look pregnant. She had done this many times. She would go to areas where they were active, and wait for them to find her. They expected her, and wanted to find her. She was one of their most popular people.

Two of the cadres couldn't be found. Perhaps they had been captured. Tho had a large payroll to deliver. What if she just didn't come back? If the cadres had been captured, or deserted, who would know? She hatched a plan to use Tet as a cover, and finally get out of this God-forsaken red dust!

First Day of Tet

Cooking the bacon in the green can would be dangerous. If the splatter caught fire on the hibachi, it would go out of control and burn down the house. Jim and Aunt set the hibachi in the middle of the dirt road in front of the house. There were no vehicles on these roads, just foot traffic, so they wouldn't be in anybody's way. Meanwhile, Tuc worked with a large borrowed mortar and pestle to grind the leaf marjoram into a powder. She devised a method of spinning the pestle between her hands, to quickly grind the marjoram. Jim had said she would need at least two large pho bowls to make the stuffing. Uncle had whittled two halves of a coconut to make something similar to pot holders. Jim started cooking the bacon. It didn't have to be crisp, just cooked. It didn't take long for bacon fat to start spattering. Jim took the coconut halves and removed the can from the hibachi. There would be too much fat. Aunt got another can to store excess, and neighbors asked for some too. Back to cooking the bacon. Aunt put some stones on the coals of the hibachi so it wouldn't cook so hot. In forty-five minutes, the bacon was cooked, and the remaining fat stored off.

Nu took Jim's knife, and began slicing the bacon

into very small pieces. When that was done, she set it aside near the roof of the house, to keep neighborhood dogs from stealing it. She fished out the stones from the hibachi, and started a large iron kettle boiling the coulan. It would take most of the day to boil enough. When each batch was cooked and soft, Jim took it and mashed it with sugar, marjoram and cayenne. He had to keep adjusting the spices as the pot got deeper. Eventually, he started adding bacon. It was delicious. Nu, Aunt, Uncle and Tuc tried it. They all grinned. "This will really be popular, Jim! We've never tasted anything like this."

By mid-afternoon, people started coming by to wish a happy new year. Each brought a bowl, and got a large spoonful of the stuffing. As they went around the neighborhood, they would get just a little chicken or rabbit or other specialties at different homes. Eventually, everyone would wander around with a bowl and sticks to visit and eat wonderful food. Jim and Nu took their bowls and wandered around. It wasn't long before they were stuffed. Aunt and Uncle took Tuc around. Some people had rice wine. Jim tried it and spat it out. The skin on the inside of his mouth felt like it was peeling. The wine was strong! This was the first time he had seen alcohol in An Tuc.

Sing!

Rose came by, and brought her guitar. "Let us quietly practice a few songs before we go to market. We can stand on a table there so people can hear us better."

"I think we can stand on a table to keep from being crushed by the crowd!" They laughed, and went over their notes. Tuc would sit on the table at the market so she wouldn't get crushed. She was excited. When they were ready, they went to the market, picked out a sturdy table, and crawled up.

Rose handed the guitar to Jim to play an instrumental before they started to sing. Jim played "Grandfather's Clock" to warm up, and "Malaguena De La Rosa", then handed the guitar to Rose. She sang a Vietnamese love song, and everyone around hushed to take in her wonderful voice. This was not one that she had practiced with Jim, so he had no part. Next, she sang one that they had practiced together. Jim sang a doo-wop type of accompaniment, being essentially the drums of an a cappella group. The crowd had grown to the point that the people in back didn't hear much at all. With no radios, this was the only music that the people of An Tuc could get to hear.

Nu signaled from below that the priest was coming with his teachers. Jim took the guitar, and waited with Rose until the priest got close. Jim started picking the tune to "Dominique." At the end of the coda, Rose and Jim started singing:

"Dominique, nique
Nique s'en allait tout simplement
Routier pauvre et chantant
En tous chemins, en tous lieux
Il ne parle que du bon Dieu
Il ne parle que du bon Dieu

A l'e poque ou Jean-sans-Terre
De' Angleterre etait Roi
Dominique, notre Pere
Combattit les Albigeois

Dominique, nique, nique
S'en allait tout simplement
Routier pauvre et chantant
En tous chemins, en tous lieux
Il ne parle que du bon Dieu
Il ne parle que du bon Dieu

Certain jour un heretique
Par des ronces le conduit
Mais notre pere Dominique
Par sa joie le convertit

Dominique, nique
Nique s'en allait tout simplement
Routier pauvre et chantant
En tous chemins, en tous lieux

Nu

Il ne parle que du bon Dieu
Il ne parle que du bon Dieu

Ni chameau
Ni diligence il parcout l'Europe a pied
Scandinavie ou Provence
Dans la sainte pauvrete

Dominique, nique, nique
S'en allait tout simplement
Routier pauvre et chantant
En tous chemins, en tous lieux
Il ne parle que du bon Dieu
Il ne parle que du bon Dieu

Enflamma de toute ecole filles
Et garcons pleins d'ardeur
Et pour semer la Parole inventa
Les Freres-Precheurs

Dominique, nique, nique
S'en allait tout simplement
Routier pauvre et chantant
En tous chemins, en tous lieux
Il ne parle que du bon Dieu
Il ne parle que du bon Dieu

Chez Dominique et ses freres
Le pain s'en vint a manquer
Et deux anges se presenterent
Portant de grands pains dores

Dominique, nique, nique
S'en allait tout simplement
Routier pauvre et chantant
En tous chemins, en tous lieux
Il ne parle que du bon Dieu
Il ne parle que du bon Dieu

Dominique vit en reve
Les precheurs du monde entier
Sous le manteau de la Vierge
En grand nombre rassembles

Dominique, nique
Nique s'en allait tout simplement
Routier pauvre et chantant
En tous chemins, en tous lieux
Il ne parle que du bon Dieu
Il ne parle que du bon Dieu

Dominique, mon bon Pere
Garde-nous simples et gais
Pour annoncer a nos freres
La Vie et la Verite

Dominique, nique
Nique s'en allait tout simplement
Routier pauvre et chantant
En tous chemins, en tous lieux
Il ne parle que du bon Dieu
Il ne parle que du bon Dieu"

As they sang, the teachers chimed in, and even the priest was smiling and mouthing the words.

Jim whispered to Rose, "Plasir." He played the first verse on the guitar, and they sang.

"Plaisir d'amour ne dure qu'un moment
Chagrin d'amour dure toute la vie
J'ai tout quittee pour l'ingrate Silvie
Elle me quitte et prend un autre amans
Plaisir d'amour dure qu un moment
Chagrin d amour dure toute la vie
Tant que cette eau coulera doucement
Vers ce ruisseau qui borde la prairie
Je t'aimerai, me repetait Silvie
L'eau coule encor, elle a change pourtant
Plaisir d'amour ne dure qu un moment
Chagrin d'amour dure toute la vie"

Rose had decided to complement Jim's bass voice by chording a counterpoint in her highest octave. It made an eerie ethereal sound, and the crowd gasped with delight.

Rose sung two more Vietnamese songs, and kept the guitar to accompany Jim on "Love Me Tender." Jim jumped off the table while singing, and wandered in the crowd, putting his arm around some of the older women, and smiling while he sang. It was a trick that Elvis had used, and it worked in Vietnam as well.

Rose asked if anyone had a request, but only a few people actually knew a song. She sung two more that people wanted, and promised to return tomorrow night.

Second Day of Tet

Everyone slept very well that night. It had been a long day, and everyone was full of good food and good cheer. Half of the stuffing was left, and had been covered for the night. Even without refrigeration, it would keep another day. Today would be easier without having to cook all afternoon. After a light breakfast that included Jim's stuffing, they all went down to the river, bathed, and then back to bed to rest a little longer. There would be no work to do this week, and with the later hours they were keeping, everyone was relaxed and tired. This would be a week for rest as well as visiting and having fun.

Around mid-afternoon, Nu and Tuc took Jim farther around the neighborhoods to visit people they hadn't seen the day before. There were lots of tasty treats to try as they walked around. Jim received lots of compliments on the singing of the night before.

With all the excitement the previous night, they hadn't bathed before going to the market, and it had been too dark to bathe after the singing, so they had gone to bed sticky. Nu suggested that they bathe before going to market today. They would still work up a sweat, but it wouldn't be as bad.

As they were leaving to go to their bath, Rose arrived,

carrying two guitars this time. "I borrowed another guitar, so we can both play. You prefer to pick, and I prefer to strum."

"Thank you, Rose! We should practice before we go to market. We were just going for our bath, but should have time to practice when we come back. Would you care to join us at our bath?"

"Thank you. I felt sticky last night. It is a good idea to bathe first."

At the river, Rose first took off her clothes, because she wore a knit shirt and khaki shorts that wouldn't dry like the traditional Vietnamese silk. She hung them on the shrubbery, and waded into the river. Trying not to be obvious, Jim compared Rose to Nu. He had grown accustomed to seeing Nu's emaciated stick figure. Rose was about the same height, and very slim, but not emaciated like Nu. Her breasts were small, but firm and high. Jim thought she could easily be a model as well as a singer. Though slim by American standards, Jim felt fat in comparison. He remembered when Tuc had patted his belly and said, "Mop." Yes, here in Asia, he could be considered fat.

Back home, Jim offered Rose some of his stuffing. "Wow! This is really good! What an exotic flavor!" Jim beamed with pride. They took their guitars, and tuned them together. "Since you pick, you can do the melodies, and I'll strum accompaniment, Jim. You can start with the melody, and after one coda, I will join in, strumming for a second coda, and then we can sing." They tried one song, and it went well. Picking up their guitars, they went to the market, where people had already started to gather around the table that was their makeshift stage.

The Red Girl

Though she had stopped at the river to wash her clothes and bathe, Tho hadn't been able to wash out the stain of Pleiku's red dust. Her clothes were still heavily stained, as was her skin and hair. That stain would never come out of her clothes, and her skin would be stained until she shed many layers of skin cells. She stood out in the crowd, and only one look was necessary to tell people that Tho was not from around An Tuc. Tet was a good cover for her, since there were many people who were just in town for the festivities.

Tho was enjoying nibbling on treats as she worked her way through town. She had worked out a story to tell. She would say that she was a student in Pleiku, but was on her way home to Bong Son for Tet. Bong Son is a coastal city, north of Qui Nhon. It was far enough from An Tuc that she wouldn't have to worry about meeting someone who could challenge her story. Though she was a Viet Cong paymaster, she wasn't high enough in the hierarchy to know what the Viet Cong plan was, or what was happening at that moment in cities all across the country. She carried the undelivered payroll money strapped around her belly, and looked pregnant.

Nu

Hearing the music, Tho worked her way through the crowd, trying to blend in as best she could. She was hearing songs in Vietnamese, and also in French and English. The English surprised her. When she got close enough to the makeshift stage, she could see that there was an American man singing with a Vietnamese woman in French clothes. She started asking people about this unusual sight, and learned about the American schoolteacher. This information might be useful to her.

Third Day of Tet

An early morning bath felt good. After breakfast, the family was just resting and talking about the people they had met and the things they had learned from all the visitors. Tet was fun, but it was also a week of quiet and resting. In many ways, it was like the Christmas and New Years holiday week in America.

"I am hearing a lot of airplanes and helicopters, Jim. Something must be happening. I hope war is not coming here."

Nu was right. Jim had been hearing more aircraft than normal. The flight pattern at An Khe did not bring aircraft directly over An Tuc, so the sound was normally in the distance, and ignored. Today, there was no letup. Just a constant drone of aircraft. "I should go to An Khe to get my mail. I'll write a couple more letters and go there. Perhaps I can find out what is happening." Jim had taken up Nu's use of the word "perhaps". He got out his paper, and wrote a couple of letters to home. As he changed into his American clothes, they heard the rumble of a convoy of American Army trucks on the main road. He decided to walk to An Khe rather than take the motorcycle.

Nu

Walking through the town of An Khe, several more convoys passed. They were traveling fast, and the soldiers were wearing full battle gear, with helmets and flak jackets. They all had their rifles in hand. Something was happening indeed.

He walked toward the main gate of the base, and saw that the perimeter was heavily guarded. He was stopped and questioned at the gate, but allowed to enter. He decided to stop at Tony's office on the way to the post office.

Entering Tony's office, Jim found Tony and John in full battle gear, with .45 caliber sidearms, rifles, knives, helmets and flak jackets.

"What's going on, Tony?"

"There's a major offensive all over the country. Fighting in the streets of Saigon, and we've lost half of it. There's a Viet Cong flag flying over the Citadel in Hue. It looks real bad. All the major cities are under full attack. The South Vietnamese Army is on leave for the Tet holiday, so we can't count on them for help. Keep your ass down!"

"Thanks, Tony."

Jim picked up his mail and went back home as fast as he could. He stopped to tell Rose the news, then he stopped at the church to tell the priest. He ran home from there, and told Nu, who spread the word. They decided to continue with the Tet festivities, but to observe curfew. Except for the police, nobody in town was armed.

They had relied on the police and the proximity of the American base.

When Nu returned, Jim said, "We have to plan."

"Yes. We need a language that you and I can use that others won't understand. German?"

"Yes, German will be good. As soon as you hear me speak German, pay attention to what is going on around us. Remember the German word for caution?"

"Yes, vorsicht."

"Good. Now, if we come under attack, since we have no weapons, everybody should run in different directions. Hopefully we can make too many targets, and more of us can get away."

"That sounds like a good plan. I will explain to the town."

"No, Rose is going to come early and we will sing. Explain it then. We will all be home by dark tonight, and be listening carefully. You can explain before we sing, and then again at the end for those that missed it at the beginning.

"Good."

"When you speak to them, ask them to set up good communications with their neighbors in case anybody sees something suspicious."

Scary Night

Less than a third of the town came to the singing tonight. The priest and his teachers didn't appear. Everyone appeared nervous. So far, there was no problem in the An Tuc or An Khe area, but that could change. The information Jim brought back from the American Army was the first that anyone had heard about the offensive.

Nu explained that since we had no weapons, the best could be done to protect as many people as possible would be to scatter in all directions, making targeting difficult. She said gathering in large groups would make it easy for the Viet Cong. At that, the crowd thinned out immediately.

"That worked. They listened."

Everyone soon went home. Bedtime was early, but most people didn't sleep much. All ears were focused on any sounds outside. There were no convoys at night, but aircraft flew all night. Flares lit up areas around the base and town. It was only a little reassuring to see the glare of the flares. Tuc cuddled tightly against Jim, who tried to lie very still. When daylight came, people used their night chamber pots rather than venture up onto the flats, until they saw that others were going to the flats.

Jim asked Nu to check in with the priest, since he had a radio. Jim would go to the base and see what he could learn.

The base was still on full alert. Jim had to wait for the normally open gate to be opened for him. He went to Tony's office first. Nobody was around. Then he tried the post office, and picked up his mail. The clerk said that information was coming slowly, but there was a long list of cities that were either under Viet Cong control or where control was dubious.

Jim remembered the list of names that Nora Hadley gave him. They were Red Cross people. He asked where the Red Cross office was, and walked five minutes from the post office to get there. He found two people, Bud Rogala and Gene Weeks. They were very busy with a huge pile of telegraph paper from the Comm. Centre. When Jim introduced himself, Bud leafed through his pile of paper, and handed Jim an inquiry from his family. Jim smiled, and wrote a response back on the bottom, saying "I'm fine. Nothing happening up here. Only the cities are affected." Bud said, "Thanks, that handles one. We didn't know how to reach you."

Jim thanked them and said he wouldn't trouble them when they were so busy, but would stop back in the future. Then he remembered, "Nora Hadley sends her regards." Bud and Gene smiled and continued working. They didn't look like they had any sleep in days. As Jim walked out, he saw a large poster by Gene's desk with Goldie Hawn. Gene just said, "Ex-girlfriend."

To Qui Nhon

Tho had slipped quietly out of An Tuc, and headed east, toward Qui Nhon. Her mind was racing. Where would she go? How would she hide? How could she get rid of the red stain on her clothes and skin. She would need new clothes. That shouldn't be a problem, since she still had the Viet Cong payroll strapped around her belly. She hadn't been to Qui Nhon, but it was supposed to be a very large city, so it should be easy to hide there. She thought it was about 100 kilometres. That would take several days. She didn't dare take the road, but had to keep it in sight to guide her. That meant traveling through the forest.

Since she was only a Viet Cong paymaster, not a fighter, she didn't have the survival skills of a fighter, but tried to figure out what the fighters would do. She decided that if they were going to observe the American convoys or to ambush them, they would have to be close to the road. She would stay pretty far from it. In that way, she hoped to avoid both the Americans and the Viet Cong. She felt very alone. She was scared. Second thoughts about her actions were haunting her.

She had to travel in the daytime. She couldn't see

where she was going when it was dark, and she couldn't see the road to guide her at night. She crossed a small stream. She was thirsty, but didn't have anything to boil the water. She would have to take her chances that it wouldn't make her sick. She took a long drink, and felt better. She didn't stop long. She had to make time, and get to a lower altitude where she could find food growing. It might take days.

At dark, she found some dense foliage to hide in. She didn't sleep well. There were no mosquitoes in this very dry area, but she was afraid of running into any humans. At this point, she had no friends. All humans would be her enemies until she could assume a new identity. What would she say, if she ran afoul of an American patrol? A Viet Cong patrol? A South Vietnamese patrol? She made up many stories in her mind, and found fault with each.

She was on the move at first light, moving quickly east. From time to time, she got a glimpse of the highway to reassure her that she was on the right track. When she was going downhill, she broke into a run, but walked up hills. Moving so quickly, she failed to see the seed. The U. S. Army planted listening devices to detect movement in the forest. She crested a slight hill, and ran down the opposite side. Near the bottom, she heard a loud "KA-RUHMP!" It was followed by many more. The explosions were in a pattern behind her, near the seed that she hadn't seen. She ran up the next hill, and found some dense foliage to hide in. Her heart was thumping wildly. She nestled into the foliage as tightly as she could. In thirty minutes, the artillery stopped, but she heard the characteristic "THUMP, THUMP, THUMP" of approaching helicopters. She sprung up, and ran as fast as she could, to the east. She wanted to put lots of distance between herself and the Americans. She heard fifty caliber machine gun fire coming from the helicopters behind her. She had no idea that they were "softening up a landing zone." She ran faster. She ran until her legs couldn't move any more, and she dove into some foliage, with her lungs straining for air. She hurt all over from the panic run. She had to force herself to be as quiet as possible. Overhead, gunships plied the sky, occasionally firing at suspect patches of jungle. They didn't come as far as she had run. What had she done to attract all this attention? She had a new appreciation for the risks her cadres took every day. She felt guilt for having taken their payroll. She didn't have to run, she chose to run. She wanted to go back, but knew that she'd be killed. Her own Viet Cong were now her worst enemy. She could never go back.

Hungry For Information

Everyone in An Tuc was hungry for information. So far, all they knew of the Tet Offensive, was the news that Jim brought back from the American base at An Khe yesterday. They continued to hear lots of air activity, and at night the flares lit up the sky. The Vietnamese police were in full battle gear, and had set up a dispersed front on all corners of town. The market was open, but did little business. Everyone was staying close to home and the little feeling of safety that home provided. Without weapons, the only real protection was the small police force and the proximity of the American base. Should town be attacked, would the Americans come to help?

Jim first walked to the church. What would the priest know? He wasn't much help. He was sitting by his radio, listening to reports in French, but the signal faded in and out. He said the reports were very bad in the cities.

Jim next went to Tony's office. John was back there, and said that Tony was attending a briefing at headquarters, but Jim could wait to see what he learned. Jim went to the mess hall next door and got some coffee for himself and John. When Tony came in, he was smiling. He sat in the chair and complained to Jim, "You got yourselves coffee, and forgot me?" They all laughed, and Jim offered to get him a cup. "No, a beer will do." Tony reached into a little electric refrigerator next to his desk and offered them each a beer. "No thanks Tony, I don't care for the stuff."

Tony began, "Well here goes. Charlie is solidly in control of Hue, and holds parts of several other cities. He has set up V.C. flags over the Citadel in Hue, and has set up a provisional government."

Jim chimed in, "So why are you smiling?"

"Because he's right where we want him. This time, he is on the inside, and we've got him surrounded. This is more like conventional warfare, which we are very good at. Charlie has thousands inside Hue, and he can't get out unless he goes to heaven. Hue is a city full of history, and we don't want to destroy it, so we're just sitting there until Charlie runs out of food. This will take a while, but we want to take the city, not destroy it. The same with the other cities where Charlie is. They changed their strategy, and the one they adopted is one that we are very happy with. Instead of small groups of sappers in the jungle that disappear into the night, we've got them cornered in big groups. Why, Hue is a corral, and the cattle are inside the gate." Tony's hat was on the back of his head, his hands were clasped behind his head, and he looked very pleased indeed.

"So what about places like this?"

"Wasn't important to Charlie. He wanted to take the cities. We're fine."

The Sgt Major was grinning now too. He fully understood what the Colonel had to say. He had been a soldier all his life, and this made good sense to him.

"Our townspeople are very worried. How much of this can I share with them?"

The Colonel winked, and said, "I wouldn't have told you anything that couldn't be shared with them."

Jim said he understood, and thanked Tony and John.

Jim didn't stop at the church on his way home. When he crossed the bridge, several students came running to get the latest news. He took them in tow, and went right to Nu. The news brought great relief to everyone. It was too late to re-start the Tet holiday, but this was good news indeed, and a semi-festive calm settled on An Tuc.

An Khe Pass

Tho started moving before first light the next day. She moved farther south, hoping to put more distance between herself and the helicopters. She again turned east, and moved very fast. She was tired, thirsty and hungry. Cresting a rise, she could see the coastal plain below. That gave her hope. She started down, but the hill soon became a cliff, so she turned north, and began looking for a way down. Gradually, she moved both north and down. She heard a waterfall, and moved toward it. When she got to the falls, she had to go up a ways to fit through a cave that the falling water had carved out of the cliff. She took her chances and drank from the falls. The water was good. She wanted to shower, but had the money taped to her belly, so she walked past the falls, and found a large flat rock. She carefully hid the money behind the rock, and returned to the falls.

Behind the main falls, she found water falling that was not so strong, so she stepped into the falling water, and felt the grime falling off her. She rubbed her clothes, and tried to get the red stain out. It would take a lot of scrubbing. If only she had some soap. She took her blouse off, and rinsed it, wrung it, rinsed it again.

Laying it aside, she rubbed herself until her skin turned red from friction. Then she took off her black silk pants and repeated the process. "This will be my best chance to get rid of the red stain." She decided to spend the night there and bathe more that night and in the morning. She drank more. "If I drink water, my stomach will feel full." She found a hidden spot to sleep, and slept well.

In the morning, she showered again, dried off, and taped the money back to her belly. Moving along the cliff, she soon came to the highway. There was no other way down the cliff, so she walked down the switchbacks toward the valley below. At the bottom, she was about to turn into the jungle below the cliff, but a jeep came up too fast, and she wasn't able to hide in time.

Geoff

After breakfast, Geoff decided to drive into Qui Nhon to pick up some supplies. The Kiwis hadn't been very busy lately, and were happy to get a little time off. This would be a good opportunity. He pulled away from the hospital tent and drove the short distance to the highway. As soon as he turned, he saw a pregnant woman walking next to the road. He tooted his horn, and pulled up along side her. He was wearing a white shirt, khaki shorts, and a baseball cap. He wasn't armed. "Qui Nhon?" Tho shook her head and smiled. Geoff patted the passenger seat, and Tho hopped in. Geoff spoke passable Vietnamese, and asked where she wanted to go in Qui Nhon.

Tho wasn't prepared for this, and didn't know if this man was going to turn her in. "Market, xin". She shook her clothes as if she wanted to go purchase new clothes. Geoff smiled, and sped towards the city. Tho noticed that he had a Red Cross insignia on his shirt pocket. Good. She relaxed. He seemed friendly enough.

Geoff thought Tho might be afraid of him. She didn't seem very conversant. As he drove, he tried to assess her without being too obvious. Her skin was the wrong color, and her clothes had a red cast too. What really made him curious was that she wasn't really pregnant. The bulge on her belly wasn't in quite the right place when she sat down on the seat, and it wasn't properly rounded. He guessed that she had something rectangular under her clothes. When she was standing, her blouse would hide the corners, but when she sat, they were visible. He decided not to confront her, in case she had a weapon hidden. He would take her to Qui Nhon.

When they pulled into the central market, Tho thanked him, smiled, and got out of the jeep. Unknowingly, Geoff had given her good cover. Tho walked purposefully as Geoff pulled away. She would need to find a place to hide the money, then come back for some new clothes. She turned south, and left town, following Highway 1 along the coast. Pretty soon, she came to a cliff on her right, and a narrow strip of beach on the left. She found a thicket with coconut palms, bananas, and other fruits growing wild and plentiful. She quickly ate several bananas, and broke a coconut on a rock, and ate it's meat hungrily. She felt better. Exploring the thicket, she found a place to hide the money, and took just enough for a meal and some new clothes. One blouse and one pair of silk pants would do, and new rubber shower clogs. She went back to the market. After getting the clothes, she immediately returned to her thicket hideaway on the beach. She would wait till dark, bathe, then discard her stained clothing. Tomorrow, she would explore Qui Nhon. It was a larger city than she had imagined, with many fishing villages, a seaport, and a peninsula farther out in the South China Sea. It looked like a nice place to live. She could start a new life here.

Nu

Geoff had returned to the hospital, and related his story about the pregnant woman who wasn't pregnant to Nigel. "I think your hitchhiker was a V.C. The Americans have detected movement in the pine forest above the An Khe Pass." The Kiwis were neutrals, and weren't armed. They would treat anyone who came in. They didn't participate in the war, so this was just passing interest.

"That would explain why she looked so odd. Her skin and clothes were stained red. She probably came from the Pleiku area."

A Quiet Time

"I am very glad that you know so much about science and economics. Nanny didn't teach me much about them, so I didn't know where to start on those subjects. It is too bad that we have no electricity, because I'd love to have you teach us all about it. We had electricity in Saigon, but all I knew of it was that it made our refrigerator and television and lights work. I never really thought about the telephone needing electricity. I dream of the day when we can have these things all over Vietnam. I'd love to have a radio or television. I'd love to speak with my father whenever I want. I'd call him every day!"

"I can at least plant the seed by teaching about modern city life, and show students with an interest what electricity can do for the town. It may be years before we can get electricity up here, but one or more of our students might take the initiative to start a power company. Electricity costs money to generate and to bring lines from Qui Nhon, but if we had enough interest, we could get people to invest in a generator, and we might start with little projects like a town freezer where perishables like fish could be stored. A radio in or near the market would be a good idea too."

"That would give us practical experience in economics too! Imagine the possibilities of learning economics while making wonderful projects that would benefit everyone! Lets start tomorrow by presenting this as a team project for the economics team. If they show interest, we can bring in more team members from the engineering and management teams."

"Excellent! We can take them to the church to see the generator, then to the restaurant to see the freezer. We can explain that perishables like meat and fish can be kept for months and even years if we keep them cold."

Nu and Jim went to sleep, each considering how to present this idea to the economics team, and which engineering students to bring into the discussion.

Life was returning to normal, following the Tet Offensive. Many thousands of people had been killed in the major cities, and there was a lot of damage to be repaired, but the small towns like An Tuc had been unaffected. When newspapers appeared in town, there was much interest in the reports from the cities. The Viet Cong had disappeared after the huge losses they incurred during Tet.

A New Life

Tho had spent days in her hidden grove, washing herself at night in the South China Sea. She would come out at night, wade into the salt water with her soap, and scrub with soap and sand. Gradually, her skin returned to its normal color.

When she felt that she had gotten rid of the last of the Pleiku stain, she decided to start a new life. She had to have a good cover story, and decided to become a prostitute for the American soldiers. That would explain why she didn't have a need for money. She started by going to cafés frequented by Americans, and observing how other prostitutes plied their trade. She would need a place to work, in a certain neighborhood that the soldiers would go for that purpose. Listening, she learned the going rates for her new occupation and the lingo that prostitutes used. She found a small storefront where she could live and do business. She paid a month's rent and moved in. It was a Spartan house, with just a bed, a table and some chairs. It suited her new trade and provided her with a home. She wasn't pretty, but she could learn how to attract needy soldiers. She would sit in front of her home, reading a book, and when soldiers would pass, she would call out, "Hey G. I., you wan boom boom?" Business was slow at first, but she gradually built up a clientele. She had her cover story.

She didn't feel comfortable hiding the money in her home, and didn't trust that it would be safe hidden in the grove that she had been using. One day, she noticed that there was a bank in the center of town. She couldn't bring that much money all at once, but decided to make small, regular deposits, in amounts she thought appropriate for a successful prostitute. She opened an account with a small amount of money. She was actually earning a good income from prostitution, and added small amounts of the Viet Cong payroll to it when she made deposits. She had never had the problem of too much money before. It was good, and at the same time it was frightening. As the weeks passed, her confidence grew. She was getting recognized and thought of as a local. This could work. She bought a small scooter and went exploring Qui Nhon and surrounding towns. She liked the coastal climate and the scenery. She made a point of not making friends, and avoiding conversations that might generate difficult questions. She cut her hair shorter, started wearing makeup and clothes appropriate for a prostitute. Her new persona was that of a successful businesswoman.

Winds Of Change

Months had passed since Tet. The country had been very quiet. Nu and Jim had gradually expanded their classes, and had many more students. Jim was becoming fairly proficient in the Vietnamese language, and to a lesser degree the Mandarin language. Nu was very comfortable speaking English with the same accent that Jim used. She could also imitate a southern accent, New York and Boston accents. They laughed a lot. It was now summer, and one day Jim pointed out Nu's shadow. It was directly underneath her at mid-day, and very tiny. "I've never seen such a small shadow." The sun was directly overhead. In America, Jim had never seen the sun directly overhead.

A gray dust settled on everything. The westerly winds seemed to blow harder every day. It was hot. Even the Vietnamese complained of the oppressive heat, and most had lived in An Tuc their whole lives. Nu told Jim that she had a very uneasy feeling. "Something is wrong. I can feel it. I am nervous all the time. I'm not sure what is bothering me, but I feel very bad."

Sluicemaster called a town meeting before dinnertime. He looked concerned. "The river is running dry. We have had no rain in three years, and the mountains that feed this river haven't had any rain in a long time. The heat and the wind are taking all the water. Our rice is not ready for harvest, but we won't be able to bring it to harvest unless we turn off the water to the distant fields, so the nearest fields can have all the water. We must begin harvesting the distant fields for the little yield we can get from them, and I will divert the water to the nearest fields in hope that we can get some yield from them. There will be no water in the bath area of the river. To bathe, you will have to go above the top sluice."

Jim said that he would go to the American base and see what the Air Force weather people were predicting.

The next morning, before it got unbearably hot, Jim went to the base, and directly to the airport. Entering the Flight Service Station, he walked up to an Air Force Sergeant and asked about the heat and wind.

"Sir, there's a monsoon coming to Asia. A deep high pressure has been building over the Bay Of Bengal in the Indian Ocean. The outflow of that high is causing this wind, which is flowing downhill over the mountains. As that air compresses, it heats up."

"Just how hot is it?"

"Right now it is one hundred twelve. Yesterday it got to one hundred twenty two. It will be warmer today. We can't use fixed wing aircraft above a hundred ten in this valley because the runway is too short and the air is too thin. No lift."

"Is there any relief in sight?"

"Not until the high pressure breaks down. That could be a long time."

"Is it this hot all over Vietnam?"

"It is hot, but not this hot. Along the coast, the water is moderating the heat, but it is hotter than normal even there. This just happens to be the worst place because of the wind funneling down from the Mang Yang Pass, near Pleiku. We've got more problems, too. Convoys bringing water up here from the desalination plant in Qui Nhon are overheating as they climb the An Khe Pass. They can only travel at night, and they're still breaking down. Water is rationed, and only for drinking. No bathing."

On his way back to An Tuc, Jim stopped at the church. There were no children in the school yard. There was only a hastily written sign on construction paper that said, "Ferme." Inside, Jim found the priest, dressed as always in his clerical robe. Jim thought it odd that he never was seen without the clerical robe. It must be his sign of authority. Jim had known priests in America, who would go to the beach or go golfing, dressed like anyone else.

"Our well ran dry. Is there water in An Tuc? "

"We have several wells, but the last one went dry Thursday."

Jim discussed what he had learned from the Flight Service Station. The priest said that he had been in An Khe for over thirty years, and had never seen it this hot before.

Passing the market on the way home, Jim found it

deserted. It was about nine o'clock, and already too hot for people to be in the market.

Sluicemaster was talking with Nu and several students when Jim got home. Nu looked up at Jim as he entered. "We have to go to the police. The remaining rice needs to be harvested or it will be ruined. It can only be harvested at night. We have to convince the police to allow a night harvest."

The small group walked the four minutes to the police station. The sun was on their backs, and burned their skin even at this early hour. Two of the police officers came out to talk, and readily agreed to the plan. They would set up a perimeter around the fields, and allow the night harvest. They would also allow night market. They asked Jim to notify the American base to expect night activity. He agreed.

It was already too hot to walk to the base, so Jim started the motorcycle, and rode slowly toward the base. Jim expected that the breeze of the motorcycle would be cooling, but at these temperatures, it felt more like a blast furnace. He was allowed to drive the bike directly to the Provost Marshal's office, and explained the situation. The Lieutenant said that he would be at the evening briefing at headquarters and let them know to expect night activity. He then handed Jim a field radio, and said to turn it on when the harvest started, in case there was a problem or any questions. Jim thanked him and went back home.

Drinking tea, Jim complained of the taste. Nu said that since the wells ran dry, they had to use field water, which was surface water. To make it safe, they boiled it much longer. "Also eat lots of fruits and coconut for water. I'm sorry, that is all there is."

Just before sunset, most of the people of An Tuc gathered at the rice fields. Many had never worked rice before, and had to learn how to harvest. It would be very hard work, especially in this heat, but it must be done to ensure rice until the next harvest. Nu told Jim to go with a South Vietnamese policeman, since he had the radio. It made sense to him. He might learn something new, because the policemen didn't mingle with the residents of An Tuc.

The policeman handed Jim a "greasegun". Jim knew it was a weapon, but it looked like a homemade weapon. The policeman showed Jim how to use it, but cautioned that it would knock Jim down if he used it on automatic. "Very strong! .45 caliber bullets." He demonstrated using verbal sounds, "POP POP POP!" and showed how the gun would jump up with each pop. Then he said, "POPPOPPOPPOPPOP" to indicate automatic fire, and showed how the gun would jump all the way up past vertical, and knock Jim to the ground. Jim now had a radio to the MP's and a machine gun. He wasn't comforted. The policeman didn't stay in one spot very long. They kept walking around the perimeter of the rice fields. With no light, Jim didn't understand how the harvesters could see what they were doing. There were no flashlights, or even candles. Candles wouldn't have worked in this wind anyway. The harvesters worked until an hour after sunrise, when the sun got too strong. Jim gave the greasegun back to the policeman, and went home. They would sleep until it got too hot. This entire procedure lasted another five nights. Everyone was exhausted, but they had enough immature rice to feed the town until the next harvest, if rain came soon.

A Bad Time For Tang

The Tet Offensive had been a disaster for the Viet Cong and for Tang. Two-thirds of his forces had been killed, captured, or deserted. With little more than couriers from the various parts of Vietnam, just taking inventory of his human and financial assets proved futile. Even couriers disappeared. The few who got back to Saigon had to rely on memory, for fear they would be caught with written information.

If the huge Viet Cong losses weren't distressing enough, Tang faced an even more distressing realization, that North Vietnamese General Giap had moved several divisions of North Vietnamese Regulars into the area between Hue and the Demilitarized Zone. These were well-trained and seasoned troops who had defeated the French at Dien Bien Phu. They moved in with tanks and heavy artillery, and the fight in that area would take months. To Tang, this meant that the North was serious about defeating South Vietnam. This was the worst possible news. Though the Viet Cong and the North Vietnamese were both committed to removing the government of South Vietnam, Tang did not want the Communists to take over. He feared that he would have to fight not one, but two governments at the same time.

Tang could not be sure which of his Viet Cong associates was a pure Nationalist and which was Communist. He had many associates that he half-trusted, but he couldn't identify any that he completely trusted.

Even Hotter

Each day seemed hotter than the last. The wind kept rising, and fruit was puckering on the trees. There had been no airplane or helicopter activity at An Khe for days. It was too hot for the air to provide lift for the aircraft. It was too hot for Jim to think of walking or riding to the base. Everyone was suffering from dehydration and exhaustion. Jim had doubts that they would survive. In his heat induced delirium, Jim was thinking about the waterfall where he and Nu had showered the day they went for mushrooms. Discussing it with Nu, she thought that the waterfall must have gone dry too.

Around noon, there was a distant rumble. It could be artillery. It could be thunder. It got louder by the minute. When the sun disappeared, they ventured out, and saw the massive thunderclouds to the west. Everyone was outside now, praying that the clouds would open and bring them rain. Sluicemaster hurried past, heading toward the main sluice above town. His workgroup followed right behind to learn what he was going to do. The thunder was very loud now, and people were smiling. The first drops of rain started to hit the ground, and there was shouting all over town. Then, the heavens opened up, and large hailstones began to pelt everyone. The stones stung, but still people were standing in the open, enjoying the welcome relief.

When the hail stopped, the rains thundered down, quickly cooling everything. People put out pots of all description to capture the rain, even the chamber pots. People turned their conical bamboo hats upside down to capture the rain, and drank from them until they could hold no more. Many people shed their clothes and stood naked in the thundering rain, enjoying the total relief they felt.

At the upper sluice, the Sluicemaster and students closed the sluice and removed the temporary dam they had made to divert water. If there was a flood, they didn't want the rice paddies to be washed away. Flood water now could once again use the river channel. Not much water yet flowed in the river, but it was muddy. Not good for drinking or washing. When they had reversed the diversion, they returned to town.

Too Much of a Good Thing

If rain is a good thing, then there was too much of a good thing. By sundown, everyone had goose bumps from the cold. It was still raining very hard, and conversation was difficult. The dust of the past weeks had turned to mud. Families huddled together to keep warm. The river continued to rise, and the paddies filled with water. It is good that the rice had been harvested, because it wouldn't have survived the hail.

For five days, the rain thundered down. The river rose above its banks, and threatened to wash out the bridge. The police bunker melted and disappeared. Some of the lower houses washed away, and their residents sought refuge with other families. Now there was water to make rice and tea. This was water that could be drunk without boiling.

On the sixth day, the rains let up in the morning, and by noon the sun was shining, and the air was fresh and cool. Jim guessed that the temperature had been below ten Celsius during the rain, and was now about twenty Celsius. Spirits rose.

Nu

Sluicemaster headed out to check the rice paddies with his team and the engineering students. It wasn't too bad. They had removed the diversion in time, and there was only minor damage to the levees. That could be repaired quickly. He wanted to get the paddies ready for planting a new crop of rice. If they planted right away, there would be time to get a full harvest. Silt that washed down would have replenished the soil with nutrients.

The Grove

Tho drove her scooter into the grove where she had hidden the Viet Cong payroll. After the Tet offensive, things had been very quiet, and she had gotten complacent about hiding. Her new cover as a prostitute had worked well, and nobody had questioned her new persona. She drove the scooter right up to the hiding spot before she turned off the engine.

Dismounting, Tho first shed her clothes and ran into the sea for a swim. She enjoyed the peaceful, warm water and the solitude here. Lazily, she swam out into the sea for quite a distance, but was still able to put her feet down onto the hard sand beneath her.

After an hour of swimming and relaxation, she walked back to the scooter, put her clothes back on, and dug out the package with the remaining payroll. Taking a small amount, she folded it and stuffed it into her clothes, and neatly wrapped the remaining payroll to re-bury.

As she bent to re-bury the payroll, an angry voice called her by name: "Tho! So that is what happened to the payroll!" She had been caught! She dropped the money, wheeling around to see three armed Viet Cong from Pleiku, pointing their rifles at her.

"I tried to pay you, but you didn't come for the money! Then the Americans came, and I ran from them! Everywhere I looked, there were American soldiers, so I kept running until I got here. I was so scared!" Tho's heart was beating so fast, she thought it would burst right out of her chest. Desperate, she tried to think of anything that might get her out of this situation. The men weren't saying anything. Finally, she blurted out, "There is an American school teacher in An Tuc, next to An Khe. He lives there. He is not a soldier. You could take him." It was all she could think of to say.

"Give me the money." Tho bent, picked up the package, and handed it to the man.

"Go!"

Relieved, Tho grabbed the handle bar of her scooter, and quickly headed towards the road. As she neared the pavement, a single shot rang out.

Golden Days

While teams worked to repair the damage to levees, others sprouted new rice plants and carefully placed the little plants across the paddies for the new crop. It was a lot of work, but there should be plenty of water for a very good harvest in a few months. This was the first rain in three years, and the mountains to the south had received enough rain to ensure that the river would remain full for a long time.

Since the rain, the temperature had remained cool, making the hard work easier. Nu and Jim were enjoying this weather. Tuc's energy level had increased, and she followed Nu around all day.

Gradually, the rice was planted, and the students left the fields to return to their studies and projects. They were glad to have planting behind them and get back to learning. The cooler weather meant that they would have more time to devote to schoolwork.

Jim arranged to borrow a truck from the Army motor pool at An Khe, and field trips were planned. Over the next two months, groups of students visited the New Zealand Red Cross field hospital, the Cao Dai Temple, and the city of Qui Nhon. For many of the students, this was the first opportunity to actually see electrical appliances, a bank, a post office, telephones or even the South China Sea. When they went to Qui Nhon, they shopped for fish and other perishables that were not available in the mountains. The students were ecstatic to see these wonders, and started planning to get a truck or bus so they could engage in trade with Qui Nhon.

On one trip, Nu was able to reach her father in Saigon by telephone. She brought the students into the phone booth, one at a time so they could see for themselves how voices could travel such distance. Nu was finally able to introduce Jim to her father over the telephone. Her father's English was very good, and they had a short but good conversation.

With each new group of students, they made a point to visit the docks, so the students could see the foreign ships from many countries, and the goods they brought to Vietnam, and the goods they took home. Qui Nhon had always been a major seaport and resort, and still was. Jim would identify the ships by nationality. Nu explained that the famous explorer, Marco Polo used to dock at Qui Nhon, to purchase tea, noodles, silk and rubber to bring back to Europe. Jim took questions on commerce and trade, tying in banking after their visit to the bank. Whenever possible, they tried to get local experts to give a talk on the subject at hand.

Whenever they stopped at the Kiwi Red Cross hospital, the doctors would give them a long talk, and give them checkups. In particular, the doctors spent a lot of time explaining the malaria parasite, and how it worked. In addition, they talked about sanitation, water treatment and waste disposal. Taking Jim aside, they mentioned that since the failed Tet Offensive, it had been very quiet, and they were planning to change their mission to visiting small towns like An Tuc and running day clinics. Jim said that would be very welcome, and asked that they let him know in advance so he could publicize it.

Useful Information

Truong Nhu Tang answered the knock on the door at his Saigon home. It was a courier, returning from delivering payroll in the northern half of South Vietnam.

"Tang, we found out what happened to the Tet payroll for Pleiku. The paymaster had fled to Qui Nhon, and still had some of the money. She also told us that there was an American schoolteacher living in An Tuc, near the American base at An Khe. I don't know how useful that might be, but that is what she said."

Tang thanked the courier, and gave him a large package, with instructions for his next trip.

By day, Tang was president of a legitimate Saigon bank. It was a good cover for him, and gave him access to all the resources he needed for his Viet Cong activities. He was indeed a man that led two lives. As a bank president, he was considered above reproach. He had access to people in all levels of government. What he did not have was access to Americans. The information he had just gotten from the courier might lead to that access. He would have to plan well. Travel was not a problem, because he had business with banks in many parts of the country, and could travel any time he wanted.

A Happy Time

"You are smiling. You look very happy."

Jim opened his eyes, and saw Nu smiling back at him. Tuc was asleep next to Jim. Aunt and Uncle were awake, lying quietly next to Nu at the head of the bed.

"Yes, I am happy."

"Tell me what makes you so happy."

"You make me happy. And Tuc, and Aunt and Uncle and our students. I never dreamed that teaching could be this much fun. I feel like we are a family, and that the students are a part of our family."

"But we have nothing. Just a few books to share. No classroom, no blackboard. There is no electricity or water or telephone. Don't you miss your American family?"

"Of course, I miss them. But I am here now, and have this wonderful family that welcomed me. They chose to bring me into their family, and to share their lives with me. They didn't have to do that, but they did. And you taught me a new way to teach, using workgroups. Your teaching style really works."

"What are schools like in America?"

"You have seen the French school. American schools are much like the French school, but there are twelve grades, rather than six. Students work alone, each with his own books. The subjects are taught the same, year after year, with a new class of students. There is almost no opportunity for students to follow their own interests, or to deviate from lessons written many years ago."

"Twelve years of school must make the students very smart, like you!"

"No, it makes us very bored. There's probably only two years of actual learning, and ten years of sitting in a chair. I was very bored. My mind was busy thinking about other things. I learned much more from just talking with adults out of school than I ever learned in school. I did learn to read in school, and I learned mathematics, and American history. Each day, I would rush home from school to read books. I learned a lot from my friends' families when I would have dinner with friends. They were doctors and lawyers and engineers and investors. They would teach their children a lot at dinner, and I was always eager to learn too, so I got lots of invitations to dinner. I think I learned most of what I know from that rather than from school. I've learned more working with you than I ever learned in school!"

"You make me very proud, Jim. I do not think I deserve such compliments. You arrived here knowing all about science and engineering."

"But I didn't learn about engineering at school. I

learned that from reading books and solving things that I wanted to understand. As a little boy, I took everything apart to learn how everything worked."

"Jim, school isn't to teach you everything. School is only to teach you how to learn. How to do research, and find out what you really want to learn. You learn some skills in school, but you learn how to work with other people to learn their skills. I think your schools must do that very well."

Arrested!

Jim and Nu were teaching algebra to a small group of students at the market, when an Army jeep pulled up. The soldiers tackled Jim, shoving him face down in the dirt. In an instant, he was handcuffed, and his knife was confiscated.

"What are you doing here?"

"I'm a teacher here."

"What unit are you with?"

"I'm a civilian school teacher. I live here."

"You can't live here. This is an unsecured area. We're taking you in to An Khe."

"That's good. They know me at An Khe. Let me get my passport and change into western clothes."

"Where?"

"I live two blocks across the road."

As they put Jim into the jeep, he noticed the stenciling on the jeep's bumper: "B CO 504 MP."

"You guys aren't with the 173d, that's why you don't know me. Where are you from?"

"Pleiku. We're the people that patrol Highway 19. Think of us as your version of the State Police."

"Okay, the Provost Martial in An Khe has a contact card on me and can clear this up straightaway." Jim guided them to his house, with Nu following behind, on foot. "You'll have to take the cuffs off for me to change and get my passport." The cuffs came off, but the MP's kept their guns aimed at him as he changed into shorts and a white shirt. Jim grabbed his passport and some letters he had written that were ready to be mailed. An MP took the documents and put the cuffs back on Jim.

Nu didn't like the way the MP's were treating Jim, and wanted to give Jim status so he would be treated better. "Wait! Jim, if you go to the Officer's Club for lunch, would you bring me a steak?" It was a brilliant move, establishing a connection between Jim and the status of the Officer's Club.

"Yes, I'll be glad to. I'll also ask Col. Herbert to join us for lunch next week." With that, he had reinforced the connection, and also acknowledged Nu's attempt to give him status with the MP's.

It was just a five minute ride to the base at An Khe. Jim was disappointed that there was a new Provost Martial that he didn't know. Jim smiled at the Captain, and introduced himself. "Hello, Captain. I'm Jim Flannery, the schoolteacher in An Tuc. You'll find a contact card on me in your Rolodex.

Nu

The Captain reached for the Rolodex, and asked if there was anyone who could identify him.

"Yes, Tony Herbert, your Inspector General, or his Sergeant Major, John Bittorie."

"Colonel Herbert is in Bong Son now. He's the C.O. of 2nd Batt."

"Okay, I've found the contact card on you. Hey, you've been here a long time!"

"Must be over a year now."

The Captain ordered the MP's to take the cuffs off. They turned to go, and Jim turned to them asking for his passport, letters and knife. His belongings were returned to him, and the MP's left.

The Captain spoke: "You must know that we can't protect you in An Tuc. You're completely on your own out there."

"Yes, I understand that. It is a great town, and we've never had any problems."

"Were you there during Tet?"

"Yes. We didn't have any problems during Tet. We were concerned when we learned what was happening in the cities, but nothing happened here."

Jim conversed with the Captain for a little while, then went to the post office and P.X. He remembered Nu's request, and stopped at the Officer's Club before leaving, and cooked two large steaks with garlic. Nu hadn't really meant for him to get a steak, but he wanted to show his gratitude and surprise her. While he grilled the steaks, he drank a Kahlua Mai-Tai. It tasted good, and took the edge off today's experience with the MP's. Wrapping the steaks in foil, he happily walked back to An Tuc. First, he stopped at home, giving the steaks to Aunt, before going back to market. He wouldn't say anything to Nu about the steaks, but would enjoy her surprise when she got home for lunch.

Entering the market, Jim was mobbed by students wanting to know what had happened after he was taken away in handcuffs. Jim was having fun laughing about the situation when Nu ran over from another workgroup.

"Nu, that was a brilliant move you made, asking me to bring you a steak from the Officer's Club. The police were much friendlier with me after that."

"I am happy that worked. Did you see Tony?"

"No, Tony isn't here any more. Now he works in Bong Son. He probably won't come back here."

"That is too bad. I like Tony. He is one of the biggest people I have ever seen, but he is so nice to us. It is time for lunch. Shall we go?"

Jim said nothing about the steak. "Yes, I'm hungry."

Walking into the house, Aunt was smiling as she sliced the steak into long, thin strips to have with pho. Nu immediately smelled the steak and garlic. "STEAK! JIM!" She turned and threw her arms around Jim's neck, hugging him hard. She had never hugged him before, and it felt good. Jim hugged her back, and could feel every rib. He hadn't thought much about Nu's emaciated body recently, but feeling her ribs and spine was a shock. He was glad that she would have a good meal.

Tuc also hugged Jim. There was seldom any meat to eat, and this was a rare treat for her. Aunt and Uncle acted like this was a special holiday. They all ate slowly, savoring the steak.

"I would like to post some letters and try to call my father. Would you take me to Qui Nhon next week?"

"Yes. We can stop to visit the Kiwis and see when they might come to An Tuc."

"Good. Let's make a day of it and visit Nora as well. And we can gather some mushrooms at the waterfall."

She May Owe Money

Jim had dressed in his western clothes to go to Qui Nhon, and they left very early before the heat of mid day. It was probably a mistake, because the sun was directly in front of them, low in the sky. The sun reflected off the layer of hot air just above the asphalt, and blinded them. They decided to stop first at the Kiwi's field hospital while the sun climbed higher in the sky.

Geoff asked if next Saturday would be a good time to come up with his Medcap. Nu said they would advertise it. "Do you have any people in An Tuc that are very sick right now?"

"A few with malaria, and some very old people with pain. Also some people with bad teeth."

"We can help with malaria and pain. We aren't equipped to drill teeth, but can remove bad teeth."

"That will help. Our hospital is just an empty building without electricity or an operating theatre. We don't have doctors or nurses there, but you can use it. There are about 20 rooms. You should bring your own water, because we only have well water. We will make food for you."

The sun was higher in the sky now, and the rest of the ride to Qui Nhon was much easier. Going to the post office first, Nu posted her letters, and tried to call her father. He was at the hospital, but was with a patient. She left a message that she called, and that she had posted letters to him. "Jim, my father hasn't seen Tuc in about four years. Tuc was too young then to know him, and doesn't remember him. I am worried that she will grow up never knowing our father. She looks to me as her mother, because she never knew our mother. My heart hurts." Jim understood, but there was nothing to say.

"It is almost lunchtime. Lets try to see Nora." They rode the motorcycle to the base where Nora worked, but were told that she had completed her assignment in Vietnam, and had gone back to America. They were disappointed.

"Let's find a café, we can have an early lunch and stop for champignons on the way back."

Riding away from the base, they found a café, ordered coffee and bun cha giao, a noodle bowl with salad, crispy egg rolls and nuouc mam sauce. It was delicious, and they ate slowly. Not far away, they saw several young men force their way into a storefront that had been closed. The men only stayed a minute, and left the door open when they ran out. Nobody tried to stop the men.

Leaving the café, Jim drove slowly past the storefront, while Nu looked inside. They didn't stop. "There was only a bed, a chair and a table. I think a prostitute lives there. She may owe money to someone." Quietly, they drove out of town toward the waterfall, their stop for mushrooms and a refreshing shower.

A Man Wants
To See You

Pulling into An Tuc with a large bag of mushrooms, Jim and Nu saw one of their students running toward them, looking upset.

"What is wrong?"

"Jim, a man wants to see you. I think he is Viet Cong."

Jim and Nu looked at one-another without speaking. Their faces couldn't hide the shock and alarm they felt. Turning back to the student, Jim just said, "Tell me more."

"I went west toward Pleiku to get pine," he held out a bag full of pine needles, "and some men stopped me. They said they want to speak to the American teacher. They had guns, but didn't wear soldier clothes. They said you should drive slowly until they stop you."

"How far out of town were they?"

"Maybe ten thousand metres. Past the Montagnard

town, and past where the woodcutters gather firewood. The pine forest is very thick there."

"How many men were there?"

"Three men that I saw, but there could have been more."

Nu said, "You can't go. They may kill you."

Jim thought a long moment. "If they wanted to kill me, they could have come here to do it. I think they want to talk for some reason. If I don't go there, they will probably come here at night. That would put everyone in danger. I think I should go."

"Then I will come with you."

"That is not a good idea. If I don't come back, you can go to the Army and tell them what happened."

"No! I will come. You don't speak Vietnam well enough to hear a nuance."

"Tanh, we will go. If we aren't back in a couple of hours, go to the police and ask them to contact the American Army."

"Yes. I will."

Nu climbed on the motorcycle behind Jim, and they rode slowly out of town, and past the American base. The Montagnard village passed on their left, then the dirt road into the forest that the wood cutters used. They continued, slowly, and passed an American convoy going the opposite direction. The road continued to climb as they continued west, and the air cooled. They were climbing to the Mang Yang Pass, which led to Pleiku.

"We've gone too far. It can't be this far, or Tanh would have mentioned the Mang Yang Pass." Jim turned the bike around, and they headed back toward town. "I think that where we passed the convoy is where we will find the Viet Cong."

You May Call Me Lee

As they neared the spot where they had passed the convoy, Jim downshifted the motorcycle and slowed. Near a drainage culvert, a man stood up, and indicated that they should hide the bike there. He then led them up a thin trail into the pine forest for about a half hour. The man didn't talk, but he didn't take Jim's knife either. Nu and Jim were aware that there were men behind them as well. They were led into a small clear area between several large pines, where a makeshift office had been set up, using logs and pine boughs. A young man stood up, and offered his hand. He was wearing western traveling clothes, and looked like a traveling businessman. He welcomed them in Vietnamese, and asked them to sit. Another man brought bowls of tea.

"Cha?"

"Cam ong." They accepted the refreshment, and waited to see what this young man wanted.

The young man was speaking softly, directly to Jim, but in Vietnamese. Nu interrupted him in English: "I know that you can speak English. Please do." Nu used a firm voice that was just short of challenging. She would not be intimidated. Jim was shocked that Nu would be so bold.

The man turned from Nu to Jim, and said, "You may call me Lee."

Nu again interrupted, "Your name is Tang. We have met before."

"Where did we meet?"

"At the University. You lectured on banking. Tang, we know who you are, but we don't know why you want to talk with Jim. Our conversation will be much easier if we say exactly what we mean."

Tang again turned to Jim. "Yes, my name is Tang, but you should refer to me as Lee. I have important things to discuss with the Americans, but I don't want them to know my real name. That would be very dangerous for me." Tang was unarmed, and soft spoken. The other men had moved away, beyond earshot, but were heavily armed. Jim and Nu had no doubt that they would kill them if Tang said to do so. Jim noted that Tang was well-mannered, well manicured, and dressed as a businessman. He is not what you would expect of a Viet Cong.

Jim was grateful to Nu for establishing openness with Tang. He was also amazed at how gutsy this tiny waif of a girl was. Taking the cue from Tang, Jim spoke. "All right, Lee." Jim emphasized the false name, so that Tang would understand that he was cooperating. "It will be easier for me if I fully understand what you have in mind, and what you want me to do."

Tang spoke: "Do you know that there are different kinds of Viet Cong?"

"Yes. Some are Communist, and some are Nationalist."

"That is correct. I am Nationalist. As Nu said, I am a banker. I am a Capitalist. There are things happening since Tet that have me very worried. The Saigon government has always been a very bad government. Our leaders fight only for their own power, not for the good of Vietnam. That is why the Viet Cong try to take over. North Vietnam has been helping the Viet Cong, but has promised that we would be free after the war. I have always doubted that promise. Many Viet Cong believe it. During Tet, we lost many Nationalists. Now we see North Vietnam preparing to change the war and we know that they want to capture South Vietnam. We can't let that happen."

"I understand what you are saying, but I don't know how Americans fit into this. What can the American Army do, and what do you want me to do?"

"I want you to find someone with authority who will talk with me. Someone who can negotiate."

"That wouldn't be the Army. They don't make policy. I think it would be our State Department. The Army only follows orders that the State Department has formulated. I have no idea how to talk to the State Department."

Nu broke in: "There is an embassy in Saigon, and another in Dalat. Is that the State Department?"

"I don't think so, but the embassy would be closer to the State Department than the Army. The Army could give me transportation, and perhaps help set up a meeting at the embassy. Lee, how would you meet with them if I could set something up?"

"I go to Paris and Geneva on business frequently. I could meet them there. I would need to meet them separately, not as part of the South Vietnam delegation or the Viet Cong delegation. Obviously, I can't let the Viet Cong know that I am meeting them, because we have many Communists. It is even more difficult for me within the Viet Cong than it is with the Saigon government."

"So you can't trust Saigon, and you can't trust the Viet Cong either?"

"Exactly. That is why you must call me Lee."

"Help me understand something. When you go to Paris or Geneva, do you represent the Viet Cong or do you represent the South Vietnamese government as a banker?"

"South Viet Nam. As a banker, I negotiate financial relationships with the banks of many governments. So you see, there is danger for me from every direction."

"I understand. This will be very difficult for me. I don't know where to start, and I don't know people who have enough authority to make this happen, but I will try."

"I believe you, Jim. If you are not able to do this, I will understand."

Nu broke in, "Where will you start, Jim? Tony?"

Jim faced Tang. "Colonel Tony Herbert is the only person of any authority that I know. He is in Bong Son. He may be able to help, but you should know that as soon as he knows about you, he will come after you. He commands a battalion of the 173d Airborne Brigade."

"I will not be here. I will be gone as soon as you leave me. I understand that they will try to find me."

"How will I contact you, Lee?"

"You won't. I will contact you." Tang stood up and offered his hand. "You have been honest with me." They shook hands, and another man came to guide Nu and Jim back to their bike.

Nu spoke first. "We must find Tanh before he goes to the police." Jim nodded, and gradually twisted the hand throttle of the bike to maximum. They didn't slow down until they had the road to the American base at An Khe in sight. As they approached the bridge to An Tuc, they saw Tanh standing by the bakery, looking very nervous.

"Another minute, and I would have gone to the police. I was very worried about you. Were they Viet Cong?"

Nu sidestepped the question. "We are okay, but Jim

needs to talk with the Army. There is no problem for us or for An Tuc."

Turning the bike around, Jim headed for the base at An Khe. The guard stopped them at the gate. "Sir, you can't bring that bike in here, and the little girl needs papers to enter."

Jim responded. "We need to see the Provost Martial immediately. Give us escort to the office." A soldier jumped into a jeep parked inside the gate, and escorted them to the P.M.'s office.

Trip To Bong Son

The Captain looked up as Jim and Nu entered. He could see the sweat on them, and the expressions on their faces. He put down the paperwork that he had been working on. "What is wrong?"

"We need to see Col. Herbert immediately. Is he in Bong Son?"

The Captain turned to a clerk and asked him to chase down Col. Herbert. Turning back to Jim, he asked, "What is it?"

"We can't give you all the details, but we just met with a Viet Cong and have important information for Col. Herbert. Just for Col. Herbert." Turning to the clerk, Jim said to let Col. Herbert know the nature of the information.

The Captain asked Jim to point out on a map where they met the Viet Cong. Jim did, and the Captain called Brigade headquarters on another phone. Tang would be expecting an assault, and would already be far from there.

The clerk said that Col. Herbert wanted Jim to come

directly to Bong Son, and said that he would order a chopper on standby at the airport.

The Captain hung up the phone, and said that he would drive Jim and Nu to the chopper. They left immediately, and found the chopper already warmed up and ready to take off as soon as they got there. Only Jim and Nu would be on this chopper with a pilot and co-pilot. Nu's eyes were wide with fear as they approached the chopper. Jim took Nu's hand, and they ducked well below the blades of the chopper as they ran to get in. There were no doors on the Huey chopper, just benches. Jim grabbed two flak jackets, and put them towards the centre of the bench, and patted one, as he sat on the other. Then he snapped the seat belt around Nu and himself.

"Jim! I am scared!"

Jim smiled reassuringly. "Don't worry, it is fun!"

The chopper took off, raising a cloud of dust and gravel. Almost immediately, it tilted forward, and picked up speed as it flew above the runway. By the end of the runway, trees were rushing by, closely. Nu was white as a ghost, and shaking violently. Jim squeezed her hand, and the chopper gained altitude quickly. Within a minute, they were high in the sky, and looking down directly at An Tuc. Without seeing close objects rushing by rapidly, Nu relaxed. "That is the market! There is our house!" Now Nu was starting to enjoy it. Her fear was gone. "Look! There is Tuc!" Nu was waving frantically at her little sister, but Tuc didn't look up. Tuc was used to helicopters, and had no way of knowing that Nu was above her. "Tuc Tuc! Tuc Tuc!"

"She can't hear you from up here." Jim smiled broadly.

The chopper followed Highway 19 east, until they got to the An Khe Pass, where it turned more northerly, above the coastal range, heading to Bong Son. In the distance, they could see Qui Nhon and the South China Sea. Below, the rugged mountains of the coastal range reached up towards them. "I have never been in the sky before! This is so beautiful!" Nu looked in every direction now, taking in the beauty of Vietnam's Central Highlands. "There are forests, but sometimes just flats with no trees at all. I could never have imagined something like this, Jim!"

A half hour later, the chopper flew over the South China Sea, and the pilot eased it towards the water. "Why are we landing in the ocean?"

Jim pointed out the port door and said, "We will turn and land at that airport. That is LZ English, the base at Bong Son."

"We got here fast!"

The chopper flew very close to the water, approaching the runway. Nu saw fishing boats below, and could see people in the boats. "I love this! I love this!" Nu's fear returned as they got close to the water, then the runway, and she saw objects flying by the door rapidly. She began to shriek with fear, and Jim put his arm around her shoulder to comfort her. The pilot pulled into a row of other choppers, and set down.

"John!" Nu saw Sgt. Major Bittorie running up to the chopper to get them. Nu was glad to see him. She was still shaking violently from the experience, but threw her arms around the big man's neck, and held on tightly. Jim grinned.

As usual, the Sgt. Major stuttered a greeting. "S-s-s-s-s-ir, the Colonel is waiting for you. I ha-ha-ha-have the jeep over h-h-h-h-here."

John drove them directly to headquarters, where Colonel Herbert already had a team assembled. He identified them as Military Intelligence. They didn't seem happy that Nu was invited in, but Tony assured them that he knew her well, and that she could help explain what happened. Tony asked Jim to give an overview.

"First, let me explain that Nu and I are schoolteachers in An Tuc, just outside the base at An Khe. I have worked with Nu for the past fifteen months or so. Nu speaks perfect English and most other languages too. She holds a doctorate in linguistics from the University of Saigon at Dalat. Nu was with me when I met the Viet Cong, and helped translate."

"The man we met with identified himself as Lee, but that probably wasn't his real name." Jim didn't mention that they knew that the real name was Tang. He continued, "This Lee also works for the Saigon government, and travels to Paris and Geneva negotiating deals with other governments. So he is a pretty high-powered guy, and he plays both sides of the fence. The reason he contacted me, is so that I would contact the Army and try to open up a channel for him with our diplomatic corps."

Several people tried to break in with a barrage of questions, and Jim continued, "That will all come clear, so let me finish with the overview, and then you can ask Nu and me whatever you need to ask."

"First, understand that the Viet Cong isn't one big happy family. There are Viet Cong that are Communist. The locals refer to them as 'V.C.' When the locals refer to non-Communist Viet Cong, they just say 'Viet Cong'. So this fellow, Lee, is a Nationalist. He isn't Communist. He describes himself as a Capitalist, and he is afraid that the North will take over. He doesn't like the Communists any more than he likes the Saigon regime. I got the impression that he'd prefer the Saigon regime to the Communists."

Jim continued explaining the situation, and then took questions. Some were directed to Jim, some to Nu. The questioning went on for a couple of hours. Finally, a major came in and said that they had located the spot where Jim had met with Lee, but hadn't located any people in the area. Jim asked if they could return to An Tuc, and Tony ordered a chopper to take them back.

Jim asked Tony if there was any way that Tony could arrange for Jim to talk with embassy officials. Tony stopped Jim abruptly, "I have one job here, and one job only. My job is to kill or capture Viet Cong. Beyond that, you're on your own."

Return To An Tuc

They got back just in time before curfew. Many students crowded around to find out what this was all about, but Nu just gave them a short version, not mentioning what the Viet Cong wanted. Aunt and Uncle had been worried, but had food prepared quickly for dinner. Nu gave Aunt and Uncle a little more information than she had given to the students, but not a lot more information.

Nu told Tuc that she had seen Tuc from the helicopter and had waved to her. Tuc was very impressed that her sister had actually flown in the sky. She wanted to know what it felt like, and what Nu could see from the sky. Nu beamed as she told Tuc and Aunt and Uncle about seeing the town from above, and flying over the mountains and the sea. She was very excited to describe how beautiful it all was from above.

After eating, they all went to the river to bathe, and fell into an exhausted sleep. Tomorrow, she would describe the beauty again, but to the students.

Danger!

It was useless to try to teach anything. All the students wanted to talk about was what happened with the Viet Cong, and Nu's experience in the helicopter. Nu had a lot of fun describing what An Tuc looked like from the sky. She gushed, describing the beauty of the mountains and the sea. Today would be a sort of picnic as they ate fruits and shared the fun. Nu announced that the next day we would get back to having real classes. She was talked out.

Heading home for lunch, Nu suddenly said, "Vorsicht!" and stepped directly in front of Jim, facing him. That was the "Caution!" signal they had worked out many months ago. As soon as Jim heard the German word for caution, his senses went on alert. Standing right in front of Jim, Nu was drawing his attention to something behind her. Jim immediately identified a man that was very out-of-place. He was Japanese, wearing shorts and a Hawaiian shirt. He looked very uncomfortable, and was watching Jim.

Jim laughed out loud, grasped Nu by the shoulders, and said, "Lets have some fun with him."

Nu

"Explain, please?"

"That man is Japanese. He is an American soldier, sent to spy on me. You go on one side of him, and I'll trap him from the other side. It will be great fun!"

Nu saw the twinkle in Jim's eyes, and understood what he wanted to do.

"When we get to him, greet him in Japanese and invite him to lunch."

Nu laughed too. She thought this would be great fun. They walked past the man, then Nu swung around and greeted him in Japanese. The man was horrified, and shrunk back from them. "I don't speak that stuff."

Nu grinned. "You don't speak Japanese?"

"My parents do, but I never learned it."

"Well, I asked if you'd care to join us for lunch. It will be easier for you to spy on us if you don't have to hide."

The man agreed, looking very embarrassed. "I told them that I wouldn't be able to pass for Vietnamese."

"Not even close. Lets have some lunch, and get acquainted."

Turning, Nu took one arm of the Japanese man and Jim walked behind. "Our home is just three minutes to the left. My name is Nu, and this is Jim."

"My name is Bill Sato. I am from Honolulu."

At home, Nu introduced Bill to Aunt, Uncle and Tuc. Bill looked at Jim, and said, "Tuc is your daughter?"

"No, she is Nu's sister. She is six years old. They are from Saigon."

Aunt easily fixed another bowl of Pho, some veggies and fruit. Bill wasn't good with chopsticks, so Aunt gave him a spoon.

Jim spoke to Bill, "You were sent to see if I am contacted again by the Viet Cong. I expect to be, but probably not very soon."

After lunch, Jim explained that school was only in the mornings, and that they take siesta in the heat of day. Bill thanked them for their hospitality, and said that he should get back to base. Nu invited him to stop in at any time.

"I Think You Should Go To Dalat."

After Bill left, the family settled down for siesta. It was a time to nap or just rest and have conversation. Sometimes Tuc would nap, or quietly play on the bed.

Quietly, Nu said, "Have you given thought about how you might get the Americans to talk with Lee?"

"That's been about all I've been thinking about since we spoke with Tony. I understand his position, but he won't be any help. I would need to find some sort of diplomat who will listen to me. Maybe I should go to the Embassy in Saigon."

"I think you should go to Dalat. There's an American embassy there, and it is very quiet."

"You've told me about going to the University there, and it sounds like a wonderful place. How do I get there?"

"You have two ways. You could go to Phan Rang, on the coast, then up into the mountains to Dalat. The embassy is on that road, just outside of the city, before you get to Dalat. The other way is to go to Pleiku, then south to Buon Me Thuot. Turn left at the market and that road will take you east into Dalat. Either way you go, it will take about three or four days by motorcycle. If you go there, would you bring us some coffee and tins of condensed milk?"

Jim smiled broadly, "Of course! As much as I can carry! I'll go to the American base tomorrow and see if I can get a flight there."

Nu grinned and closed her eyes.

Trip To Dalat

After a quick breakfast, Jim packed his western clothes in his backpack, and walked to the airport at An Khe. They didn't fly to Dalat, and their flight to Buon Me Thuot had already left, but he was able to get on a flight to Nha Trang and Phan Rang. The flight was on a C-130 transport, the workhorse of the U. S. military. Every one of these planes looked incapable of flying, but they were very powerful and reliable. There were no actual seats, but there were places to strap yourself in, which was a good idea. The planes were unbelievably noisy, and were flown hard.

It took two hours to reach Nha Trang, and after a short stop, it was only fifteen minutes farther to reach Phan Rang. When they got there, Jim tried to get a flight to Dalat, but was told there wouldn't be a flight there for several more days. He asked how else he could get there, and was told to try a bus downtown.

Finding the bus station was easy. It wasn't far from the American base, and Jim found a bus already loading. He purchased a ticket, and tried to climb aboard. The bus was full, but he found a seat. This bus wasn't built for westerners, and Jim couldn't get his hip bones between the armrests. People watching him try, laughed, and pointed to the roof. Climbing out, Jim climbed up a ladder on the rear of the bus to the roof, which was filled with luggage, caged chickens and ducks, and a young Vietnamese man that looked like a student. The man introduced himself as Vinh. He was a student at the university in Dalat, and spoke excellent English. Jim took up a sort of nest amongst the luggage, next to Vinh, and they talked as the bus moved slowly out of town.

Heading west, the bus strained even on the flat coastal plain. Vinh explained that the busses were always overloaded, but usually succeeded in getting to their destinations. He laughed, good-naturedly. Jim liked Vinh. At first, conversation was only possible when the bus was going slowly through villages. After an hour, they started climbing lacettes, and the road got steep. The bus often slowed to walking speed, and strained in its bottom gear. Conversation was easier at these speeds.

"Jim, I like to ride on the roof, because it is so crowded inside the bus. The smell of the chickens isn't as bad as being squeezed!"

"I've gotten used to the smell already, but the feathers in my eyes and mouth are really bad!"

"Ha ha! Maybe I can find a recipe for feathers in my books." Vinh laughed, patting his knapsack.

"What are you studying at Dalat?"

"I major in history and language, with a minor in economics. Some day, Vietnam will be the crossroads of Asia, like Singapore is today." He opened his knapsack, and started showing Jim his books. "You see this print? It is just the same as Thai print. Vietnam used this print a long long time ago. Several times, we were conquered by China, and we used print like this." Vinh opened another book, written in Chinese. "Our official writing is the Pin Yin print that the French gave us, so they could sound our words with the western characters. Most of us can also read Chinese, but only a few scholars can read the old books with the Thai print."

"Can you read all three?"

"Yes. Our history has almost been lost. The French re-wrote our history, and the children were taught wrong history. I read the old manuscripts in the original language, and I try to correct the history. I do not claim that the French intentionally changed our history. Perhaps, but I think they just didn't understand our history, and wrote it down as they thought things happened."

Jim noticed Vinh's use of Nu's favorite word, "perhaps." He avoided saying anything, because he didn't want to advertise Nu's location, in case he mentioned it to a V. C. Vinh may have picked up the word from a professor that they had in common.

"In a little while, we will come to a military checkpoint, where they will check our papers. They should not want to check an American's papers, so stay on the bus unless they ask you to come down."

Jim nodded, then thought of his knife. Patting the knife, he asked, "Should I hide my knife?"

"Put it in your knapsack. It should be all right."

The air felt cool and good. They had climbed for hours, and gained a lot of altitude. Along the way, they had passed lakes, and seen several waterfalls. There hadn't been a village in about two hours. The forest had changed from broad-leafed trees to pines, and would have smelled good if they didn't also smell the chickens. The road leveled off by a building, and the bus came to a stop.

"This is where I have to get off to have my papers checked. Pay attention in case the Army asks you to get off. The bus will be fueled here as well." Vinh climbed down the ladder, with his knapsack and papers, and stood in a line with the occupants of the bus. Jim just sat by the ladder, and smiled.

A Vietnamese soldier went inside the bus, and checked everything left in the bus. Another climbed the ladder, and checked the luggage and chickens, then climbed down. When the bus had been serviced, and the people all were cleared, the bus reloaded, and Vinh climbed back on the roof. "We will be in Dalat in an hour."

"There is supposed to be an American embassy before we enter Dalat. Would you point it out?"

"Yes. It is near the coffee plantations. I will show you. When we get to Dalat, it will be too late to travel, so you won't be able to come back to the embassy until tomorrow. I live at the university. Do you have a place to stay?"

"No, are there hotels?"

"Yes. Several hotels close to the bus station. Look, we are in the coffee now."

Jim looked at the neat rows of cherry trees that covered the hills on each side of the road. They stretched as far as he could see. He smiled, "I am going to like this. I love your coffee!"

"Yes, very strong, good coffee. There are still many French that live in Dalat. You will find that most people speak French and Vietnamese. I need my coat now. It is very cold here."

Jim had been shivering. "I didn't bring a coat. You are right, it is cold and humid."

"We have a lot of fog here. It almost never is warm. Look, there is the American embassy."

Jim looked ahead, and saw what looked like an old French plantation. It had an American flag, a concrete wall, and a small guard shack with two uniformed Marine guards. Not much security for a country at war. The building looked like it had about twenty rooms, but there wasn't much activity.

"Look ahead. This is Dalat!"

Jim looked into a broad valley, with a surprisingly large city. In the centre of the city, he saw a large lake, with a very large fountain. "Dalat looks like Geneva, Switzerland!"

"Yes, I have seen pictures of Switzerland, and it does look like Dalat. You will find Dalat to be a quiet city. It is very peaceful here, and the people are friendly."

"I have found friendly people everywhere in Vietnam." Jim smiled.

The bus snaked down into the bowl that was the city. It was getting dark, and Jim noticed lights all over the city. "Electricity! We don't have electricity in the town where I live. Or a post office, or telephones."

"We have all those things in Dalat. We will be at the bus station in a few minutes. I have enjoyed talking with you today, Jim."

"I have also enjoyed talking with you, Vinh. You have taught me many things that I didn't know before.

The bus stopped, and they climbed down the ladder. Vinh pointed out some hotels, and then the campus. "You will find many European professors here, and several American professors."

Jim and Vinh had a long handshake and wished one another well.

Looking around, Jim picked out a European-looking hotel, and entered. He registered, and went to his room.

The bathroom was a surprise. It had the usual footprints accommodation, but also had a toilet and a bidet. There was running water, and the hot water faucet provided real hot water. There was the usual sign saying that the water was not potable. Jim showered, and changed clothes to go to dinner.

The concierge recommended a restaurant directly next

door, and said that Jim should put his traveling clothes outside his door to be washed over night. Jim thanked him, and went back to the room to put the clothes out.

The suggested restaurant turned out to be an excellent choice. Jim was fascinated with a huge photo mural on one wall, showing Dalat, covered in a fresh mantle of snow. The waiter verified that it occasionally snows in Dalat. He explained that the lake lies in the caldera of an (hopefully) extinct volcano, at an altitude of 2000 metres. The surrounding mountains rise above 3000 metres, and frequently are snow-capped. He said that there is an airport, but it is 30 km south of the city, and takes an hour to get there by Lambro.

Jim noticed that half the patrons were Vietnamese, and the rest were European. The menu was in Vietnamese, French and English. Selections on the menu were both Vietnamese and continental. Jim chose coffee first, then vichyssoise soup and goulash. The soup was refrigerator cold, and tasted very fresh. Jim guessed that it was made with potatoes, leeks, cream and whole fresh leaves of a purple basil. Very refreshing, but also very filling. The goulash was delightful and very tender, served over wide flat noodles. Jim thought that the goulash gravy had been made with a generous portion of cream cheese added to beef gravy and sour cream. In addition to paprika, there was a hint of cayenne, to give the dish a little zip. The result was a heavenly treat, but Jim pushed half the noodles off to one side, since he was already full from the vichyssoise. The waiter was very professional, and spoke English and French without difficulty. Jim left a generous tip.

The Embassy

Jim rose early, and found his freshly laundered clothes neatly folded, lying on the floor just outside the door, with a local newspaper printed in French. He checked to see if there were other languages inside, but there wasn't. He decided to bring the paper back to Nu. She would enjoy reading it.

Going downstairs, he found tables set up in the vestibule with continental breakfast, consisting of baguette rolls, fresh European butter, jams, tea and coffee. He drank two glasses of coffee while eating the rolls. The butter was just like you'd find in Europe, and was far superior to American butter. He savored the flavor while drinking coffee.

Walking out of the hotel, he got a sudden chill. There was dense fog, with some cold mist. It took a minute to get his bearings and figure out which road to take. Seeing a swarm of Lambros waiting outside the hotel, he approached one. "American embassy?"

"Yes, fifteen minutes. Two hundred Piasters. You are American?"

"Yes." Jim got on board, and the Lambro lurched as it pulled into traffic. There was no traffic control, like in the rest of the country. As they climbed out of the valley, the mist turned to rain, and Jim was drenched by the time he got to the embassy.

"You want I wait? Two hundred Piasters every hour."

"Khong, cam ong." Jim didn't know how long it would take at the embassy, and didn't want a cab burning his precious money while he was inside. He had noticed many other Lambros on the road, and knew there wouldn't be any problem hailing another for the trip back.

The Marine guards were wearing ponchos, plastic caps over their hats, and umbrellas. They checked Jim's passport and let him right in. The vestibule was austere and large. The greeter was a young Vietnamese woman wearing a white ao dai, the formal attire. She looked up and smiled.

"Hello! You are soaking wet. I will get you some towels." She quickly ran to another room, and came back with two bath towels. "Can I get you some tea or coffee?"

"Hot coffee would be wonderful, thank you."

She returned with a cup of coffee, some milk and sugar on a silver service. Jim thanked her.

"What can we do for you today?"

"I need to speak with a diplomat." Jim didn't want to give her too much information.

"Do you have a passport problem?"

"No, I have information that they will want to hear. It is very important information, but of a confidential nature."

"Enjoy your coffee, and I will find an officer to speak with you."

Jim looked around. There were several chairs, and some coffee tables with magazines. He saw "Life", "Look" and "Readers Digest."

Fifteen minutes later a young, soft spoken man came to him, introduced himself, and asked Jim to come to his office. As they entered the office, Jim closed the door behind them, and took a seat opposite the officer.

"Our secretary said that you had information of a confidential nature."

"Yes. I was contacted by a highly placed Viet Cong government official, who is trying to open a communications channel with our government. He frequently travels to Paris and Geneva, and wants to quietly negotiate directly with our government. While he is Viet Cong, he is not Communist. He is afraid that the North Vietnamese will take over, and he wants to work to see that does not happen."

The officer was unimpressed. "We are already in

Paris, trying to meet with the Viet Cong on an official basis. So far, nothing is working."

"He wants to meet unofficially."

"We won't do that. Everything must be official. There won't be any unofficial negotiations with the Viet Cong." The officer was quiet, but firm. He wouldn't hear any arguments.

"You'll report this conversation to your superiors?" Jim slightly emphasized the word "superiors" to let the officer know that he recognized the officer as a low level diplomat.

"Of course."

"Then make sure you tell them who I am in case they decide to do otherwise. Here is where I can be reached." Jim wrote his mailing address on a sheet of paper, and that he could be contacted through Col. Anthony Herbert or the Provost at An Khe. The officer stood up, extended his hand, and offered to help if Jim should need any embassy services. The offer was absurdly routine. Jim had no expectation of any results from this visit.

Leaving the embassy, Jim started walking toward Dalat. In a few minutes, he flagged down a Lambro for a ride back to the city.

A Real Downer

Jim was dejected. The meeting at the embassy had been a real downer. Even the lifting sky and a weak sun did nothing to cheer him up on the ride back to Dalat. Ordinarily, this would have been a great adventure, and he would have stayed in Dalat a few days to enjoy the local sights and a visit to the campus, but he wanted to get back to An Tuc as quickly as possible. He spent the rest of the day picking up condensed milk and coffee for Nu. He had to have the coffee ground here, because they didn't have a coffee grinder at home. He decided to retire early for a quick start in the morning. He checked at the bus station and obtained a ticket to Buon Me Thuot, where the 173d Airborne Brigade had a battalion. He hoped to get a quick flight back to An Khe.

In the morning, he had time for the continental breakfast before taking the bus. It was foggy again, but no mist or rain. He was glad. This was the same type bus that he had ridden to get to Dalat, so he went right to the roof. This time, there was only luggage on top, no chickens or company to talk with. Jim was grateful that he wouldn't have to ride with chickens. He didn't feel much like conversation today either.

Nu

The bus first climbed through plantations of coffee cherries and pine forest, to the rim of the bowl surrounding Dalat. After the rim, the road was very steep and twisty. Jim hoped the brakes would hold, and had doubts. He was prepared to jump if he had to. After an hour, he could see the Dalat airport in a flat valley below. The bus stopped there to discharge and pick up passengers, and to refuel. There was an Army checkpoint, but only for traffic going towards Dalat.

Leaving the airport, the rest of the trip was mostly through very rich farm country with coffee cherry, rubber plants, tea and fruit trees. Jim's spirits rose seeing all this beauty. Though the trip to Buon Me Thuot was roughly the same distance as the trip from the coast, it went much faster going downhill. They pulled into town in early afternoon. It was hot and muggier than An Tuc.

Jim walked through the market, noting the different foods than were available in An Tuc. He asked questions about some of the fruits and vegetables that were unknown to him. Many of the vendors gave him slices of fruits as they talked. He would have picked up some things if his backpack wasn't already crammed with coffee and tins of condensed milk.

Seeing some Army jeeps, Jim picked out one with "173" on the bumper, and asked for a ride to the base. After checking in with the Provost Martial, Jim went to the airport and asked to catch a ride to An Khe. He boarded another C-130, and strapped in. After a three hour flight, the plane banked, and went nose down into the valley, turning a tight spiral. The mountains surrounding An Khe prevented a gentle landing. The

C-130's had to screw themselves into the valley in a steep dive, and only flare out at the last seconds with full flaps applied. It was always a frightening experience, but the pilots were very good.

On the ground, Jim went directly to the Provost Martial's office, only stopping to pick up his mail along the way. The Captain looked up as Jim entered. "Well?"

"I went to the embassy in Dalat, but they weren't very interested. The officer I spoke with was a typical bureaucrat. It was just like dealing with the government." Jim grinned a wry grin, and the P.M. laughed.

"Can I try to get Col. Herbert on the phone while I'm here?"

"Sure." The Captain turned his phone around towards Jim, and motioned for Jim to sit.

Picking up the phone, Jim waited for the operator, and said, "LZ English, please." When the Bong Son operator came on line, Jim asked for Col. Herbert.

"Who are you?"

"Jim Flannery."

"Rank and unit?"

"Civilian, An Khe. Tony Herbert is expecting my call."

Jim heard the ring on the other end, and the Sgt. Major came on the line.

"Hey John, Jim Flannery. Is Tony there?"

Nu

Tony picked up the phone, and said, "Have you had any more contacts with the Viet Cong?"

"No Tony, but I just returned from the embassy in Dalat. They weren't helpful, but I told them that if they want to contact me, they can call you. I hope that's okay."

"Yeah fine Jim, but I doubt you'll ever hear from them. Gotta go. Nice to hear from you."

Jim turned to the Captain. "It is almost curfew. Can I get a ride back home so I don't get stuck on base tonight?"

"Yes. I'll drive you myself. I'd like to see where you live." They went out and took a jeep with a blue police light on top. The Captain drove Jim directly home, but didn't come inside. "Nice place." Jim chuckled. The Captain's tone really meant, "How the hell can you live here?"

Nu, Tuc, Aunt and Uncle came right out to greet Jim, and he threw his backpack on the bed. It was heavy, and landed with a thud.

"Tell us what happened!"

"It was every bit as beautiful as you described, but I have to go up to the flats for relief first. Come with me." Jim had looked directly at Nu, and his request indicated to her that he wanted to tell her about the embassy in private. He was not in the habit of inviting people to go pee with him.

Nu excitedly headed toward the flats with Jim, and Tuc followed. Tuc wouldn't understand what Jim had to say to Nu, so that wasn't a problem. As soon as they were alone, Jim told her about the bureaucrat, and his disappointing visit. "Just in case Lee contacts you and I'm not around, I want you to know exactly what I did, so you can tell him." Nu nodded, and listened. Jim explained that he had told the bureaucrat to let his superiors know of Jim's visit, and that they could contact Jim through Col. Herbert if they were interested in talking further about it.

"Yes. I understand. If Lee contacts me, I will tell him exactly that."

"We may never hear from Lee again. Or the embassy. Or Lee could contact us at any time. We won't know until something happens. We are just messengers, and can only wait to see what develops."

After relieving themselves, all three went back home for dinner and a bath before bed. During dinner, Jim filled Aunt and Uncle in on the ride to Dalat and all the things he saw on his trip. Nu backed him up on the things he told them. Tomorrow, they would repeat the conversation with the students, but not the part about the embassy visit. That was only for Nu to know.

"After seeing the mountains, the coast, and Dalat, I think that Vietnam has to be one of the most beautiful countries on Earth."

Back To Normal

After breakfast, Jim and Nu went to the market, accompanied by the usual throng of language students. The language students followed Jim and Nu to all the workgroups, and learned about each subject in addition to learning English. Those that already were proficient in science, math or history assisted in teaching those subjects. In that way, they also learned how to teach. It was the best of all worlds.

When they got to the history students, Jim had a special lesson that he had learned from Vinh, while riding on top of the bus to Dalat. He explained that the only way to be certain of Vietnam's history was to go to the cities like Saigon, Dalat or Hue and research the old manuscripts from ancient times. He told them of the Chinese and Thai writing that Vinh was using, and how the French had re-written Vietnam's history because they didn't understand it. "The French didn't mean to write your history incorrectly, but they couldn't read the ancient writings, and compiled your history from what people told them." He explained that Vietnam was distinct for over three thousand years, but that the size and shape of the country changed many times in three thousand years. "Many times in three thousand years, Vietnam was conquered by different groups of people from what is now China and Thailand. That is why you use Chinese and Vietnamese writing, and why your languages are so close. Even before the Chinese, Vietnamese people used Thai writing." Nu agreed, and said that she had learned that at the University.

Weeks passed, and there was no contact from Lee. A couple of times, American soldiers stopped to ask if Jim had heard anything more from the Viet Cong. His answer was always the same, that he hadn't heard, but that he would contact the Provost Martial and Col. Herbert as soon as he did.

Drafted!

Jim went to An Khe to pick up his mail. The clerk handed Jim a stack of letters, with a rubber band around. Jim looked at the top letter, and his heart sank. The return address was

Local Board # 52
Selective Service Commission
ENCK Bldg
Lemoyne, Pa.

"Oh shit!"

The postal clerk laughed. "Looks like you're going to have to change your clothes, Sir!"

Jim opened the letter, sitting on the steps outside the post office. He was supposed to have reported for induction at New Cumberland Army Depot, but the induction date was the day before. "Oh shit, I'm AWOL!"

Jim went right to the Provost Martial, and showed him the letter. The P.M. laughed out loud when he read it.

"I was supposed to have reported yesterday. That makes me AWOL. What do I need to do, surrender to you?"

Still laughing, the Captain said, "Well Jim, you could do that, but I'd suggest that you use my mill," he pointed to the typewriter, "and write them a letter. I'm a Notary, so I'll put my seal to it, and give you a cover letter to send along. I think we need you right here in Vietnam." He was grinning broadly.

By now, Jim was also grinning broadly. "Yes! Thank you!" He wrote a letter back to the draft board, and the Captain put his seal on it, and wrote a letter of his own. In the P.M.'s letter, he explained that Jim was not only teaching school, but also assisting the Army in gathering "local intelligence." Jim shook his hand hard, and ran back to the post office to post the letter.

When Jim got home, he handed the letter to Nu. She read the letter, and looked up. "I don't understand. What is this?"

"I've been drafted into the Army. They want me to go back to America so they can train me to come here."

Nu's face drained of color. She stood in front of Jim, but didn't say anything.

"I wrote back, telling them that I was already in Vietnam, and wanted to stay here. The Provost Martial also wrote a letter, verifying my letter, and asking them to leave me here."

"When will you know their answer?"

"The draft board meets once a month. It may take some time to hear."

"Will you be able to stay while you wait for their answer?"

"Yes. Most of the soldiers would rather be at home, but I would rather be here. The Provost Martial thinks they will let me stay."

"I am relieved, but tell me as soon as they answer."

"I will. Would you like to go to the Chinese restaurant tomorrow for some chateaubriand?"

"Oooooo, yes!"

Just then, there was a commotion outside. They listened to hear what was going on. Jim asked, "Who died?"

"Nobody died, it was a water buffalo that died. Tomorrow, the whole town will have meat for lunch. Preparations are being made for a big fire to cook the meat. It will have to cook all night because water buffalo are so big. We should wait to go for chateaubriand."

The fire was set up at the edge of the market, while a team of people worked to cut up the buffalo to bring it to the fire. It was a long, thin fire, made with charcoal. Rocks were placed amongst the coals, to elevate the meat above the fire. The meat was wrapped in large leaves to let it steam and to keep flies off the fresh meat. The police were notified and invited to the feast. They would allow people to tend the fire tonight. Such a large fire would take a lot of work to maintain.

Feast

The aroma of the cooking meat wafted through town. There was an air of anticipation in a town that seldom had any meat. The students kept eyeing the fire during morning classes, waiting to hear the call that would indicate the meat was ready.

"They do this in Hawaii with pigs, and call the meal a 'luau.'"

"I like pig. That would taste good."

Instead of pho today, people cooked rice, coulan and other root vegetables to go with the buffalo. When the smaller pieces were thoroughly cooked, they were unwrapped from their leaves, and momentarily dropped onto the hot coals to brown on the outside. The browning meat smelled better than when it was steaming. Large plates collected the meat, and families came by to slice pieces off the meat on those plates. Uncle asked for Jim's knife, and sliced off a large piece of meat. He then carried it home and divided it four ways.

Jim tried his piece of buffalo. It tasted pretty bad, and was impossible to chew. Aunt, Uncle, Tuc and Nu seemed to be enjoying theirs. Jim cut his into very small pieces, hoping it would be easier to chew. He almost gagged on a piece that got stuck in his throat when he tried to swallow it. He put his meat back on the family plate, and ate the rice and vegetables instead.

"You don't like the buffalo?"

Jim didn't want to insult, but admitted that he couldn't eat it. "I will be fine with rice and vegetables." He put some nuouc mam on his vegetables and took some crispy sprouts and a couple of habanero chilis. Later, when he was alone with Nu, he admitted that the buffalo tasted terrible. "I don't like the pork from a luau either."

Nu had a twinkle in her eye. "Next week we will go for chateaubriand." She smiled, and Jim showed his pleasure with a smile.

The next week, Jim and Nu walked to An Khe for chateaubriand. As they passed the church, Jim noticed several American soldiers coming out. He wondered why the soldiers were at the church. The restaurant's doorway was closed by the roll-down metal gate signifying that it was closed and locked. There was a sign written in Vietnamese, Chinese and English. "Closed for Christmas." Nu and Jim both laughed. "We missed Christmas!"

"Ha ha, we will come next week. Merry Christmas!"

Medcap

Nu and Jim had been looking forward to going to the Chinese restaurant for chateaubriand, and waited until the second of January. Just before lunch, a jeep drove into the market. It was Geoff and Nigel, from the New Zealand Red Cross. They asked if they could come in two days to do a Medcap. Nu thought that would be perfect, and suggested that they come early before it was too hot. Two days would give her time to pass the word around town through the students. The language students said they'd contact the rest, and would also assist the Medcap as interpreters.

Jim and Nu asked Geoff and Nigel to join them for chateaubriand, and they graciously accepted. The foursome went to An Khe in the jeep, and Nu pointed out the police station, bridge, bakery and Catholic church. Both Geoff and Nigel had been to the American base at An Khe, and had a working relationship with the U S Army hospital there. They also knew the Red Cross staff.

During lunch, Jim told them about the experience with Lee. Later, it would turn out to be a wise move.

Nu

The Red Cross was a neutral organization, and was left alone by all belligerents.

Over the next two days, Nu, Jim and the students passed the word across town and also An Khe about the Medcap visit. It would be at the makeshift hospital at the north end of the market. There was already a small group of people gathered when a truck rolled in carrying Geoff, Nigel, and a lot of supplies, including a generator for electricity. The Medcap lasted all day, but all the people who came were seen.

Since Nu's parents were doctors, she volunteered to assist. She was familiar with the instruments and procedures, and proved to be a valuable asset. At the end of the day, Geoff and Nigel had Jim and Nu in the back of the truck, loading equipment and drinking cold beers and pop from a refrigerator in the truck. Nigel was very pleased. He commented at how healthy the residents of An Tuc were. There was malaria, and the prostitutes from An Khe had venereal diseases, but there were no ulcers, heart or stomach diseases. "Your diet, and the simple life here are very healthy."

Nu thanked them and said that she hoped they would see them again soon. "We try to go to Qui Nhon once or twice a month for mail, and will try to stop in when we pass your hospital. Will you join us for our Tet celebration?"

"We try to stay at the hospital for Tet. We are concerned because of what happened last year."

"We don't expect a repeat of last year. Most of the

V.C. were killed last year, and it was such a disaster for them that we don't think they will want to repeat it."

"In that case, we'd be glad to celebrate with you. We will contact the Americans and Koreans to let them know to expect our truck on the highway one night."

"Koreans?"

"Yes, our hospital is inside the Korean AO. The Koreans don't cross into American areas, and the Americans don't cross into the Korean areas. That keeps them from shooting at one-another."

Motorcycle Lessons

Jim had been teaching Nu how to ride the motorcycle. At first, Nu had trouble activating the shift lever with her left foot, because her only shoes were shower clogs. One of the engineering students studied the problem and fashioned a long and wide lever from scrap metal. With the force spread out over a wider area, the lever didn't cut into her foot while shifting. After siesta, and before dinner, Nu would ride the cycle alone for a half hour each day. Jim showed her how to stand on the pegs when going over bumps, to use her legs as shock absorbers.

"I think I am ready to take Tuc for a ride, if you think I am ready."

"First, you must take me for a ride. If you can ride with my weight behind you, then you'll be ready to take Tuc."

"That is good. You are right. Shall we go now?" Nu was very excited, and it showed on her face.

Jim grinned broadly. "Yes. Take me wherever you want. I want you to practice both fast and slow, and I want you to make some turns with my weight behind you."

"Are turns difficult with two people?"

"Yes. You will see. And I want you to ride on the dirt as well as the road. You can ride on the dikes between the rice paddies."

"Ooooooo, yes! Lets go!"

Jim climbed on behind Nu, and was faced with a new problem. Nu was his friend and co-worker, not his girlfriend, so he didn't know where he should put his hands. Nu was so tiny that he had to be careful. He decided to hold her hips.

Nu's first attempt to get underway resulted in stalling the bike because of Jim's added weight. "I understand now why you wanted me to take you before taking Tuc."

The second attempt was more successful, but at slow speeds, Nu had trouble keeping the bike upright. It wobbled from side to side, and Jim said, "Go faster, and it will be easier." Nu opened the throttle, almost sending Jim off the back. The front wheel lifted off the ground slightly. Backing off the throttle a bit stabilized the bike, and all was well as soon as they approached cruising speed. "You've got the idea now. Slow speed is difficult with someone behind you. Get used to carrying me, and in about ten minutes, I want you to slow down and make some turns, to see what that feels like." Nu nodded her head in acknowlegement. Jim was glad that Nu was so tiny, because it gave him the opportunity to see over her head. "I hope I haven't been squeezing you too tightly. I'm not used to being a passenger."

"You are strong, but you don't hurt me."

Jim eased back on his grip of Nu's hips until Nu slowed down to practice turning. She slowed down, and started her turn, but was going too slowly to keep the bike stable, and ended up driving all the way off the road, into a ditch, where the bike fell ungracefully. Jim laid on the ground, laughing hysterically.

"You are not mad at me?"

"Heck no! That was fun!"

"Why do you say wrecking the bike was fun?"

"Because I knew it would happen the first few times you tried to do that. It happens to all new riders. That is part of learning how to ride a bike. That is also why I wanted you to practice on me, and not on Tuc."

"Oh! I understand completely! Thank you!"

After picking the bike up, they re-mounted, and continued eastward on Highway 19, towards the An Khe Pass. Nu practiced a few more turns, with better results. "I don't want you to drive down the pass until you are more experienced. The lacetttes are very tight and difficult, especially with the steep road."

"Okay, I will turn around by the help girls at the top."

"You want them to see you driving."

"Yes! Yes!" Nu was laughing, and thoroughly enjoying herself.

They pulled into the little aid station, and Nu proudly announced that she was learning to drive the motorcycle. There was a lot of giggling from all of them. As they were talking, the girls packed up their gear, and were picked up by a Lambro. It was the end of their day, and would soon be getting dark. Jim and Nu turned around and headed back towards An Tuc.

An Unexpected Visitor

"When we get back to An Tuc, turn onto the dikes to practice carrying me on the dirt."

Nu turned her head to acknowledge, and saw a car approaching. "There is a car passing us."

It was very unusual to see a car. The priest had one, and the Sergeant that ran the NCO Club at An Khe had one to go to market for fresh fruits and vegetables. Other than those two cars, only one or two came through An Tuc each month. "Pull to the right and slow down a bit to let the car pass us." Nu did as Jim requested. As the car passed, Jim looked inside it to see who would be driving this road in a car. The man looked familiar, and was wearing a business suit. Jim shouted to Nu, "It is Lee!" The car passed, then slowed and pulled to the side of the road. Nu stopped behind the car, and they walked up to the driver's window. It had been months since they met Lee, and they weren't sure they would ever see him again.

"Hello, Lee. I didn't know if we would ever see you again. I have much to tell you."

"Hello, Jim, Nu. I just returned from Paris. I met with an American diplomat there, but he would not negotiate with me. I think he knew about me, so you must have done something. Tell me about it."

Jim told Lee about meeting with Col Herbert and the Military Intelligence people. He also told Lee that he had gone to the American Embassy in Dalat, but had a cold reception from the bureaucrat there.

"Everything you tell me explains the conversation I had with the diplomat in Paris. That man seemed to know what I wanted, but he was cold to me as well. You are an honest man, Jim, and I appreciate that. I also want to tell you that the North is sending a lot of soldiers here, and they are taking over. I think it is too late for the Nationalists. It has become very dangerous for me."

"I understand, Lee. Thank you. If I get another opportunity to try to open up a discussion, I will do that."

"Thank you. I was going to drive all the way to An Tuc to find you. Is there anyone else I can contact if I need to reach you?"

"Yes. Before you came up the Pass, did you see the Red Cross tents north of the road?"

"Yes, I did."

"That is a group of doctors from New Zealand. They

are not political. They know me, and know how to contact me in An Tuc."

"Thank you. It will be dark soon, so I must return to the coast." Lee turned the car around and headed back towards Qui Nhon. Jim noticed a license plate on the back of the car, and it was a government plate.

"Lets try driving on the dikes." Jim grinned.

"You aren't going to the American base first?"

With a twinkle in his eye, Jim said, "It may be too dark to approach the base when we get back. I may go there tomorrow. I have to think of what to tell them."

Nu easily drove back onto the road and towards An Tuc. "I wasn't afraid this time."

"I wasn't either. I think Lee is honorable."

New Base Commander

Jim walked into the Provost Martial's office the next morning. The Captain looked up, and asked, "Well, have you seen your Viet Cong friend yet?"

Jim knew that the Captain was joking, but he shocked the Captain with a simple, "Yes."

The Captain jumped up and said, "We have a new base commander. Let's go see him." They jumped into the jeep, and sped to headquarters. The Captain skidded to a stop at headquarters, and ran in, followed by Jim.

"Sir, this here is Jim Flannery, the schoolteacher in An Tuc."

The Colonel faced Jim, without offering greetings. "I know who you are. Col. Herbert told me all about you."

"I've had another contact from the Viet Cong, so you'll probably want to bring Military Intelligence in."

"Sergeant! Send Sgt. Olejniczak in here. I'll do better than that, Mr. Flannery. Sgt. Olejniczak is C.I.A."

"And he's in the Army?"

"Sure. He is a Sergeant, and he's attached to the C.I.A."

After a brief introduction, the Sergeant started asking the questions, and the Colonel and Captain observed.

"When did you see this V.C.?"

"Just before dark, last night."

"Where?"

"About one click this side of the An Khe Pass."

"Why did you go there?"

"I was teaching my co-worker how to drive my motorcycle."

"What took you so long to report this?"

"By the time we got back, it was too dark to approach the gate."

"How did this guy contact you?"

"Lee saw and recognized me, so he pulled me over." Jim didn't mention that he was driving a government car.

"What did he want?"

"He wanted to know if I was able to get someone in

the Army or the diplomatic corps interested in negotiating with him. I told him about my conversation with Tony Herbert and with the embassy in Dalat. Negotiation isn't a function of the Army, so the diplomats would be the only avenue open to him."

"How did he take that?"

"He just got back from Paris, and he talked with an American diplomat there who didn't seem to want to open up any talks."

"So this Lee is important enough to go to Paris?"

"Yes. He goes there frequently. By the way, he is Viet Cong, not V.C."

"Explain."

"He's a Capitalist, not a Communist. He wants to overthrow the Saigon government, but he's a Nationalist, and wants to replace Saigon with reformers who are not Communist. He told me that the N.V.A. is moving in, and taking over from the Viet Cong. That worries him."

"Are you leveling with me?"

"Absolutely."

The Sergeant wheeled around and left the room without saying any more.

The Colonel just said, "If he contacts you again, you come here immediately."

"Okay. Of course." Jim knew that the Colonel was used to people saying "sir", and he didn't oblige.

The Colonel didn't look happy. He addressed Jim directly: "You are here legally, and I can't do anything about that, but I consider you to be just one more thing that I have to worry about."

Without saying more, Jim turned around, and the Captain said, "I'll take you back home."

"That's okay, I need to go to the post office before going home."

"Did you ever hear back from the draft board?"

"Not yet." Jim had almost forgotten about the draft board. He hadn't picked up his mail in a couple of weeks, and rushed to the post office to see if a reply had come. It had. The draft board sent more than a form letter, and informed Jim that they considered his obligation to be met, so he would not have to be drafted. He rushed back to tell Nu.

A Thrill For Nu

Jim found Nu with the commerce workgroup in the market. She looked up and scanned Jim's face. "How did it go, Jim?"

"I just told them about my meeting with Lee. Nothing important." Then he grinned, and handed Nu the letter from the draft board. She read it, and squealed with delight.

"Oh! I am so happy!" Nu did that little dance that made her look like a skeleton dangling on strings, and Jim laughed.

Jim stayed with Nu and the commerce students until lunch, then they went home to tell Tuc, Aunt and Uncle the good news.

After siesta, Jim suggested that they visit the Kiwis to let them know that Lee might try to reach Jim through the Kiwis some day.

"Oooooo, can I drive the pass?"

"Yes. I will take you down and up, then you can take

me down and up. When I take you, watch my speed and how I take the turns."

"I will watch carefully!"

Nu drove to the help station, then let Jim drive to the bottom of the pass and back. She watched carefully, and then Jim let her take him down and up. She did very well, and Jim suggested that she go a little faster uphill.

"Now drive me to the Kiwis." Jim was smiling broadly. Nu easily negotiated the lacettes, with her confidence building. At the bottom of the pass, she turned and headed to the Red Cross tents.

Geoff came out to greet them. "I saw you going up and down the pass several times. What is happening?"

Nu answered, happily: "Jim has been teaching me how to drive the bike. This is my first time to drive the pass!"

Nigel had joined Geoff, along with two new doctors. Geoff congratulated Nu on her driving skill. "To drive that road with such a heavy load, isn't easy. What do you weigh, Jim, about 65 kilo?"

"Probably about that."

"And what do you weigh, Nu, about 30?"

"I have no idea what I weigh."

"Well, come inside, and we have a scale."

Jim and Nu each got on the scale, and found that

Geoff's guess was very close. Jim weighed more than twice as much as Nu.

"You should eat more, Nu."

"I eat all day. I don't know why I am so skinny."

"Most of the world would love to have your problem."

Jim swept the room with his hand to indicate he was addressing all the doctors. "We have things to tell you."

Nu and Jim brought all the doctors up to date on their contacts with Lee, and what Lee was trying to do. Then he told them that he had told Lee to come to this hospital if he needed to reach Jim. The doctors were very interested, and grateful to be in the loop.

Nu drove Jim back up the pass and to home. When they got home, Jim told Nu that she was ready to take Tuc for a ride on the motorcycle. Nu was so happy, that her face looked like it might crack from grinning so hard. Tuc hugged both Jim and Nu very hard.

"Before I take Tuc for a ride, I have to relieve myself so I don't ruin the motorcycle seat! Come, Tuc!" Nu and Tuc ran up to the flats, leaving Jim laughing in the doorway of their home.

Aunt wanted to know what Nu and Tuc were so excited about, so Jim explained, while drinking a cup of tea. Aunt and Uncle stood outside when Nu and Tuc came back to go for their ride. They wished Nu luck as if she was about to drive around the world. Nu beamed with delight, but blushed from all the attention.

Jim leaned back for a short nap. He wanted to look very relaxed, but felt like a father must feel the first time his daughter takes off solo in the family car.

When Nu and Tuc returned, Tuc was jumping with joy. "I've never gone so fast!" Nu just watched Tuc and smiled proudly.

"Jim, I am glad you taught me so well how to ride the motorcycle. I felt safe to take Tuc with me. I was able to show her things that were too far for us to walk." She hugged Jim, and Tuc hugged him too.

Aunt asked Jim for his knife. She used it to slice a pineapple in bite sized pieces, and set out a tray for the family and the small crowd of ever-present students. Eating pineapple, Jim told Aunt that ripe pineapples are sweet, and much better than in America.

"What is wrong with pineapples in America?"

"They are grown in Hawaii and other tropical places, so they have to be picked green, before the sugars are ready. Green pineapples taste sour and make your face pucker." Jim puckered his mouth to demonstrate.

The Challenge

For the next few weeks, Tuc excitedly looked forward to her dinnertime rides with Nu on Jim's motorcycle. The bike had opened up a whole new world for her. She had seen Montagnard warriors in town, but had never been to their village west of An Khe. Nu took her there, and translated her questions about their life. She hadn't seen homes built on stilts, and was invited to go into three of them. She found it very interesting, and Nu had to censor some of Tuc's questions, when the questions got too personal. The Montagnards were short, but much stockier than Vietnamese. They were very powerful people with a simple language. Their tribes recognized no nations or borders, so they freely migrated across Southeast Asia in search of game. They did not farm, but would steal crops grown by the Vietnamese. They didn't see this as theft.

One afternoon, Nu took Tuc to the waterfall on the An Khe Pass, and they gathered mushrooms. Then they went down to visit the Kiwi doctors before returning for supper. Tuc had never seen a waterfall, and thoroughly enjoyed standing under the cool falling water. She excitedly told Aunt and Uncle about it when they returned. She thought it would be wonderful to live in such a place. Tuc's excitement at her growing world seemed to awaken a new growth in her development, and she became hungry to learn new things.

Nu recognized this, and began taking Tuc to classes, like a regular student. Tuc's thirst for knowledge grew daily. Perhaps she needed just this sort of thing to grow out of her retardation. Nu was excited to see the change in Tuc. Her speech was still "baby talk," but now she was asking questions all the time, and she was picking up English as well.

"We won't be able to speak privately in front of Tuc any more, Jim."

"Well, we still can use German until she picks that up too." Jim's face told Nu that he was half-kidding.

"When she picks up German, we will have to speak Hebrew!" Nu laughed out loud.

Two of the older students had been spending more time with Nu and Jim for some time. Lon was in her late teens, and had a black baby that she was almost finished breast feeding. Her little boy was already eating rice and soft vegetables and fruits. Jim wondered how many Amerasian children would be left behind when the war was over.

Vu was a young man about the same age as Lon. He had managed to avoid the draft so far, but it was nearing the time when the Saigon government would come through to corral the young men for the Vietnamese Army.

Nu had been relying on Lon and Vu to assist with classes, and they had proven themselves to be both reliable and worthy.

Jim had noticed that Nu had been writing through the afternoon siestas, instead of napping. Sometimes she would write a page, then discard it and start over. That was different than when she wrote her father.

"What have you been writing that is so important?"

"It is time for Lon and Vu to take their Challenge. I have been documenting their knowledge and experience."

"What challenge?"

"Real schools give diplomas, but most Vietnamese don't have the opportunity to go to a school like the French school in An Khe. Still, they have accumulated much knowledge and skill. I never went to a real school until the University. My teacher was my Chinese nanny. I had to go to the University and pass an oral Challenge to prove my skills. It now is time for Lon and Vu to go to the University and Challenge for their teaching certificate."

"Is it that easy?"

"It isn't easy at all, but they are ready. They are knowledgeable and skilled and experienced. It will cost money, but I have been collecting money from the people at the market, and now have enough money for them to pay for the Challenge. It will take a week for each of them, in front of a board that will decide if they are worthy. Vu will have to take his Challenge before the Army comes. If he has his certificate, he won't have to go with the Army."

"Lon is still nursing her little boy."

"She says that he is ready to stop nursing. Another mother will take the boy until she returns. I wanted Vu to wait for Lon so they could travel together for safety, and to support each other. Tomorrow I would like to spend time with them to build their confidence, and to give them their letters to take to the University."

"Will they go to Saigon or Dalat?"

"Dalat. I wrote cover letters to professors that I know there. The professors already know that they are coming. I hope that the University will be able to schedule the Challenge quickly."

"They will need papers at the Army checkpoint before they enter Dalat."

Nu jumped up quickly. "Oh! I forgot!" She ran out the door, towards the police station. A few minutes later she returned. "The police will make their papers. They have to stop there tomorrow to fill out papers, but the police say no problem. They will need new clothes also, so I will take them to the tailor and tell him what is acceptable at the University."

The next day Nu would be busy with Lon and Vu, so Jim agreed to take all the classes. When he came back for lunch and siesta, he found Lon and Vu sharing the bed with Nu and Tuc. Jim decided to skip lunch and siesta, and go to the Chinese restaurant in An Khe for lunch. After lunch, he went to the American base and picked up his mail and some tins of tuna for Lon and Vu to take on their trip. They would have to take the slow busses from Qui Nhon, so the trip would take several days each way.

On his return home, Nu told him that Lon and Vu had decided to travel in two weeks, so Nu decided to send some letters to her professor friends in Dalat. "Can we go to Qui Nhon tomorrow to post my letters?"

"Yes. That will be good."

Nu spent the rest of the day writing letters, and was exhausted by evening.

A Magnanimous Offer

Nu was finishing her last letter when Jim awakened. They quickly ate breakfast, took a quick bath in the river, and left for Qui Nhon. Nu drove the motorcycle, allowing Jim to look around as they traveled.

"It is nice to have you driving. I can look around and enjoy the scenery more than when I'm driving. I can even see over your head!" Nu nodded her head in agreement. She was now quite skilled with the bike, and understood that the passenger had more freedom to look around than the driver.

With the letters posted, Nu tried to phone her father in Saigon, but he was busy with a patient.

"Lets pick up some dried fish and go home."

"Good. We can visit the Kiwis on our way back."

Pulling into the New Zealand Red Cross Hospital, they could smell the barbeque, and it made them hungry.

Geoff greeted them. "You're just in time! We have steaks today. Please join us."

As they ate, Nu told them that she was sending two students to the University for their challenge to become certificated teachers.

Nigel asked how they would get to Dalat, and Nu explained that we would take them to Qui Nhon by motorcycle, one at a time.

Geoff said that Jim could borrow a jeep from their hospital, and take Lon and Vu together.

Nu beamed, "That would be wonderful!"

"Stop here the day before, and take the jeep. You can return it and pick up the bike after dropping them off at the bus station in Qui Nhon."

That settled, they all grinned, and enjoyed the rest of their lunch. With no bus service to An Tuc, transportation was always a problem. The Kiwis were good friends, indeed.

Good Luck!

The next two weeks were a whirlwind of activity for Lon and Vu. They had lots of questions about the Challenge, and about Dalat and the trip ahead of them. On the afternoon before their trip, Jim drove the bike to the Kiwi's camp and picked up the jeep. It would be a squeeze, but Nu planned to bring Tuc along. She had written her father, and asked him to be at home so that Tuc could speak with him. Tuc had been just a baby when he saw her last, and she was now seven years old. Nu had told Tuc about their father, but Tuc wasn't convinced that he was real. Perhaps speaking with him would help. Nu was very excited! It had been a long time since she had spoken with her father too.

After breakfast, Vu and Lon came with their traveling bags, and had brought a lot of traveling food, including the tins of tuna that Jim had gotten at An Khe. They had wrapped balls of cooked sticky rice in grape leaves. It would go well with the tuna. A small amount of rice vinegar would keep it from spoiling, and they had basil, ginger, garlic and chilies to make it tasty. They would have to make do with stops at towns along the way for water in the form of tea or coffee. They had no means of transporting water. Nu had them each drink several cups of tea before leaving. Neither Lon nor Vu had ever been to a city, and were nervous.

Jim slowly eased through town, with Lon and Vu waving to everyone. There were many shouts of "Good luck!" as they went through town. Out on Highway 19, Jim sped up, and everyone's hair blew in the wind. Tuc was now familiar with this road, but Lon and Vu hadn't traveled so fast before.

Jim pulled over at the aid station at the top of the An Khe Pass, and everyone relieved themselves, and accepted a cup of tea from the aid girls.

Not far below the aid station, Nu pointed out the trail that they took to the waterfall and gather mushrooms. Lon and Vu now could see things that they had discussed. Jim pointed out the white tents with the Red Cross on top, and explained that it was the New Zealanders there that had loaned him the jeep.

As they passed the Cao Dai Temple, Nu explained about Cao Dai, and how the religious people there had set up "small temples" inside to compare the religions. Lon and Vu had heard of Cao Dai but weren't familiar with it otherwise.

Entering the coastal plain, Lon and Vu could see the city of Qui Nhon below, and were impressed with the size of it. They saw docks in the bay with large cargo ships. Their heads turned constantly from side to side, taking in all this wonder.

Jim slowed as they entered Qui Nhon. "Watch carefully, because this is the way you must come back. You will just stay on this road. It takes you right to the bus station. If you don't know which way to go, it is the only road that goes into the mountains." Lon and Vu nodded.

Pulling up at the bus station, Jim stayed with the jeep to guard it, and Tuc stayed with Jim. Nu took Lon and Vu inside to show them how to purchase their tickets. Nu returned, smiling. "They are very excited!"

Tuc was excited too. "Nu, what should I say to our father?"

"Tell him you want to meet him! Tell him how wonderful it is to finally talk with him. Then tell him anything you'd like. I will be on the telephone with you. He loves us very much. Tuc, I really miss Father. I wish that we could see him on the telephone."

Jim drove the few blocks to the post office, and Nu first checked for mail. There was a letter from their father, saying that he would try very hard to be home when they called. Nu showed the letter to Tuc, and they waited in line for a booth. Jim stayed outside to guard the borrowed jeep. He knew that the telephone system was seldom successful, but he prayed that Tuc would finally be able to talk with her father.

An hour passed, and Jim finally saw Nu and Tuc running out of the post office. Their faces told the story. Tuc had spoken with her father! She ran straight to Jim, telling him over and over how happy she was. Nu had tears streaming down her cheeks, but she was grinning. She hugged Tuc tightly, and they both laughed and cried all at once. Jim felt their excitement and could hardly contain himself. After they regained their composure, they drove back to the Kiwi camp.

"We have a special lunch for you today, that Tuc should enjoy! We have hot dogs. Kids everywhere love hot dogs."

Jim grinned, then saw that Nu and Tuc were horrified. "What's wrong?"

"We can't eat dogs!"

Suddenly, Jim understood. "Oh! These aren't really dogs. That is just a name we use. They are made from pigs."

"Why do they call them dogs?"

Jim looked at the doctors, and nobody could answer the question. "I don't know. It is just something strange in English. In German, they are called "Frankfurter Wurst", but that might be difficult for English speakers, so we call them hot dogs."

The doctors displayed a package of hot dogs, and let Nu and Tuc smell them. "You see, they aren't dogs at all. Look, here are the ingredients." Geoff pointed to the ingredients, and Nu read off the words until she got to the chemicals. She agreed to try one. Nigel put about twenty of the links on the barby, and set out buns, catsup, mustard, relish and sour kraut. Nu tasted each of the condiments, and asked if the sour kraut was kim chee.

"It is similar to kim chee. It is made from cabbage, which is like bok choy. They add salt to preserve and flavor it, and they might ferment it a little." Jim wasn't sure about the fermentation, so he looked to the doctors for help. They weren't sure either.

Jim explained that you put the frankfurter (he was careful to call it a frankfurter) in a bun, and then add whatever condiment you want. He suggested trying one bite with each condiment to see what they like.

Taking a bun, Jim put his frankfurter in it and demonstrated putting a little mustard on one bite, and some relish on the next bite, then some sour kraut on another. Nu and Tuc tried each condiment. Nu liked the sour kraut, and Tuc preferred the relish.

Finished with their hot dogs, Tuc asked if she could have another. "You can have as many as you can eat!"

All three grabbed a second hot dog, and Tuc even ate a third. Geoff addressed Nu, "You are the one that needs a third."

"But I am full! These are wonderful!"

Finishing her third hot dog, Tuc announced: "I want to tell Aunt how much I enjoy eating dogs!"

Nu's eyes glazed over with happy tears. Tuc had just demonstrated that she had a sense of humor. Nu was thrilled. Two years earlier, she didn't think that Tuc would ever be smart, but in recent months, Tuc's speech had cleared, she was speaking English, and showing interest in the classes. Now she was demonstrating humor. Tuc had spoken well to her father this day, and Nu could hear that he was very impressed with his littlest girl. There hadn't been much hope for her when she was born blue.

Nu hugged Jim, and wiped her eyes on his shirt. "Tuc is growing up. I am so very happy! I think she is getting smarter every day."

"Yes, I have noticed that. Her world is bigger than the house now. She has ridden on the motorcycle, in the jeep, and been to a city. She has met the Montagnard people, and showered in the waterfall. She just needed to be stimulated by new and exciting things. Now she wants to learn things in class. I think you should take a vacation to Saigon so she can see and touch her father, and see his hospital."

"Yes. We should do that. Perhaps we will go for Tet. Father would love that, and I miss him very much." Nu's voice cracked from emotion. This had been an exciting and wonderful day for both of them. Jim's eyes had glazed over too.

After lunch and a brief visit, Jim thanked the doctors for the loan of their jeep. Nigel said that he had filled the gas tank on the motorcycle, and Jim thanked him for that too. Just then, Jim was faced with another problem: there were now three people to ride the motorcycle back to An Tuc. The seat was barely large enough for two. Jim would have to sit on the gas tank, and put Tuc between Nu and himself for the return trip. Getting on, Nu found that she couldn't get her arms around both Tuc and Jim at the same time, so she had to hold on to Jim's belt. It wasn't comfortable, but it worked.

"If you fall off the back, yell very loud!" They all laughed.

Making Plans

They arrived home late in Siesta, and although they were all very tired, Nu and Tuc couldn't stop talking about the trip, talking with Father, and eating hot dogs. Nu had to explain that hot dogs weren't dogs at all, but Tuc was enjoying the joke, and said, "They are like dog's tails." Nu told Aunt and Uncle that she would probably take Tuc to Saigon at Tet to visit their father.

"I will have to write Father and tell him what we want to do."

"When you get to Saigon, hide the bike because it may be stolen."

"Do you want us to take the bike?"

"Of course!"

"Oh, that is a very long way to ride the bike!" Tuc had been listening, and her face gave away her excitement at the prospect of a very long ride on the motorcycle, and finally meeting her father.

Nu immediately started writing a letter to her father.

"This will be a very long letter. It will take time to write. There is so much I want to tell him!"

"You just spoke with him this morning." Jim grinned, needling. He knew that Nu wanted to tell her father things that they didn't have a chance to discuss on the phone, like a trip home at Tet, and Tuc's recent unexpected development.

After class the next day, Nu continued to write furiously to her father. By evening, she had finished, and asked to borrow the bike the next day to post the letter. She wanted to post it as quickly as possible, and not wait until after class.

"Yes, of course. I'll take the classes and you can go to Qui Nhon in the morning."

Sudden Ending

Two weeks later, Jim asked Nu when she thought Lon and Vu might be back from the University.

"If they were able to take their Challenge straightaway, they should be back any day. They might not have been able to schedule it quickly, though. Sometimes you must wait for the board to become available."

"I will feel better when I know if they passed their Challenge."

"I am nervous, too. I didn't want to say anything, and have kept busy to keep from thinking about it. We will know when they return."

Walking into the market, they were joined by the English students, who followed them to the science workgroup. The English students were lucky, because they got to attend all the other classes while learning English. It was an excellent way to learn English.

With the English and science students together, the class numbered about a hundred students. Jim and Nu had to speak up to be heard by all.

Suddenly, a jeep sped into the group, coming to a dusty, abrupt stop. It was Geoff and Nigel. They looked worried. Jumping out of the jeep, they headed straight for Jim.

"What is wrong?"

"Your friend, Lee just came to us. He says that the Communists know you are here, and are coming after you. You must leave immediately. We contacted the American Army by radio, and they said there was a North Vietnamese regiment nearby that they are tracking."

A paralyzing chill went down Jim's spine. The color drained out of Nu's face, and the students stood very silent, taking this all in.

Jim turned to Nu. "You must take Tuc to Saigon immediately. I will go to the American base."

Nu collapsed to the ground from the shock, and Nigel lifted her legs to let blood flow to her head to revive her. In a minute, she awakened, and a merchant brought her tea.

Jim addressed the students quickly.

"I have to go home to America. Nu will have to go home too. If the Communists come, you can't tell them that we were warned to leave. Just say that I went home to America. If they ask about Nu, tell them that she went to Hue. Don't say where she really went. Lon and Vu should be back soon. You have all been wonderful, and I will always remember and love you."

Nu

Nigel turned to Nu. "Get in the jeep. We will take you and Jim home to pack your things, then we will take Jim to An Khe. When you are ready to leave, come to our hospital to spend the night."

Nu nodded, unable to speak. They got in the jeep, and drove the three blocks to home. Jim quickly explained to Aunt and Uncle what had happened, while he packed up his things from under the bed. Nu was also packing, and Jim handed her his backpack for her trip. He wouldn't need to take much with him. Tuc appeared frightened. Jim hugged Aunt and Uncle and Tuc, and thanked them for two very wonderful years of their hospitality.

Jim then turned to Nu. He held her by the shoulders, and they looked into one-another's eyes. There was so much they wanted to say to each other, but nothing needed to be said. They hugged tightly for a moment. Nu had never gained any weight, and Jim could feel every bone in Nu's back. He kissed her on the forehead, and got into the jeep. As they drove away, he looked back, and Nu was still standing in the same spot, holding the backpack, with tears streaming down her face. Tuc was holding onto Nu very tightly.

Going through the gate at An Khe, the guard was expecting them. "Go immediately to Headquarters, Sir. They're expecting you."

The Colonel greeted them. "We've already made contact with a regiment of North Vietnamese regulars. There are more in the area. The First Sergeant is cutting orders right now to evacuate you from the country."

"To where?"

"San Francisco. When you get there, you're on your own. If anyone questions your orders, tell them that you were a contractor to the Army."

"Thank you, Colonel."

The First Sergeant handed Jim an envelope with many papers, and said he would take Jim to the airport.

Jim turned back to Geoff and Nigel. "Thank you for everything. You've been good friends. Please make sure that Nu and Tuc…" He couldn't finish the sentence.

"We will, Jim. Take care."

Epilogue

Nu and Tuc spent the night at the New Zealand Red Cross Hospital, and left for Saigon early the next morning.

Jim Flannery never went back to teaching, but worked as an engineer until his retirement from MCI in 2000. He wrote several letters to Nu at her Saigon address, but his letters were returned a year later, marked "Undeliverable."

Lt. Col. Anthony Herbert had made many enemies in his years as Inspector General. Several senior Army officers trumped up charges alleging that Col Herbert had covered up atrocities committed to Vietnamese civilians. He was drummed out of the Army in disgrace. CBS' "Sixty Minutes" filmed an expose titled "The Selling Of Colonel Herbert," in which Mike Wallace presented the charges against Col. Herbert as fact.

Col. Herbert and Sgt. Major John Bittorie had kept files to document and prove Col. Herbert's innocence. They filed suit against the Army and CBS, calling many witnesses, and showing their documentation. They won the lawsuit. They were able to prove that CBS had collaborated with senior Army command, including

General William Westmoreland, to destroy Col. Herbert and discredit his earlier, documented allegations.

Col. Herbert, who had a degree in psychology, spent the rest of his life working in that field.

Truong Nhu Tang (Lee) was identified as Viet Cong and captured by the South Vietnamese government. He spent several years in prison, tortured severely to make him identify other Viet Cong.

After the fall of Saigon, he was again captured, but by the Communists this time. They sent him to "Reeducation Camp" where he was tortured for years. Many of the former Viet Cong suffered this fate along with him. Eventually, he escaped to Paris. He wrote an autobiography detailing much of his life. The autobiography is titled, "*A Viet Cong Memoir*," published by Vintage Press in 1986. It can be purchased at this link:

http://www.amazon.com/Vietcong-Memoir-Account-Vietnam-Aftermath/dp/0394743091